Pete looked from child to child. "We want the spirit of these verses to pervade our home, and in light of this wish, your mother has something to say that I'm sure you will all find interesting."

From the recliner where he slouched, Mazeltov in lap, legs tossed over one arm of the chair and his body's weight resting more on his waist than his spine, Jordan called, "Yay, Mom."

Molly cleared her throat and ordered her heart to stop its unruly palpitations.

"Amie, P.J., and Jordan, I have two things to say. First, I want to ask your forgiveness for being a lax mother." She paused and took a deep breath. "And secondly, I must tell you that due to lack of respect and because of constant harassment, the maid has quit."

There was a moment of silence while the children stared at Molly as if she were crazy. Then a great wave of sound washed over her..

D0173743

MULTNOMAH WOMEN'S FICTION
ROMANTIC COMEDY

Gayle Roper

ENOUGH!

A NOVEL

Multnomah®Publishers *Sisters, Oregon*

This is a work of fiction. The characters, incidents, and dialogues are products of the author's imagination and are not to be construed as real. Any resemblance to actual events or persons, living or dead, is entirely coincidental.

ENOUGH!
published by Multnomah Women's Fiction
a division of Multnomah Publishers, Inc.

© 1997 by Gayle Roper
Published in association with Sara Fortenberry, P.O. Box 8177,
Hermitage, TN 37076-8177

International Standard Book Number: 1-59052-527-2
Previously 0-57673-185-5

Cover illustration by Paul Bachem
Cover designed by Brenda McGee

Scripture quotations are from:
The Holy Bible, New International Version (NIV) © 1973, 1984
by International Bible Society, used by permission of
Zondervan Publishing House.

Printed in the United States of America

ALL RIGHTS RESERVED
No part of this publication may be reproduced, stored in a retrieval system, or transmitted, in any form or by any means—electronic, mechanical, photocopying, recording, or otherwise—without prior written permission.

For information:
MULTNOMAH PUBLISHERS, INC.
POST OFFICE BOX 1720
SISTERS, OREGON 97759

05 06 07 08 09 — 10 9 8 7 6 5 4 3 2 1

For Doris Gordinier, my mother
and Edith Roper, my mother-in-law

Everyone should be blessed with moms like you two.

Finally, all of you, live in harmony with one another;
be sympathetic, love as brothers, be compassionate and humble.
Do not repay evil with evil or insult with insult, but with blessing,
because to this you were called so that you may inherit a blessing.

1 PETER 3:8–9

ENOUGH!

Mom, we're going to be late! We're always late. It's embarrassing." P.J. stood impatiently at the front door, arms crossed over his chest. He looked like a bouncer who was having a bad night at the club.

Molly clutched her robe tightly and grabbed her husband Pete's jacket from the closet. She slid it over her robe, promising herself that some morning when she drove one of her children to school, she'd wear clothes like real people did. Such phenomena must occur somewhere besides commercials.

"Mom!" Amie came bursting down the hall. "Where's my white blouse, the one with the bow at the neck? I have to wear it today because we're singing for the assembly."

Molly sighed. Senior Singers had proved to be one of those double-edged honors a mother could live without.

"I haven't seen that blouse since you last wore it. Why not wear your pleated one?"

"Are you kidding?" Amie's expression showed clearly what she thought of her pleated blouse. "Everyone's wearing bows. Everybody!"

"Mom!" P.J. rattled the doorknob pointedly.

Jordan loped past on his way to the breakfast table and his usual three bowls of cereal.

"Mom, did you make me two sandwiches for lunch?" he asked. "I never get enough to eat anymore. I think you're trying to starve me."

"Butt out, Brace Face," said Amie with her usual elegance. "I'm talking to Mom."

Jordan assumed a look of wounded surprise. "Mom only talks to you these days? I think not."

As Amie snarled, P.J. rattled, and Jordan pontificated, the phone rang. Everyone looked at Molly.

"Other people can pick up the phone, too, you know," she said. "Get it, Jordan! You're standing right beside it."

"But it's never for me," he said, then grabbed the phone and grunted into the receiver. How, Molly wondered, had he lived with a phone-o-phile like Amie all these years and still not learned the basics of phone etiquette?

"Hey, Dad," Jordan bellowed. "It's Pop-pop for you!"

Pete hurried down the hall from the bedroom looking unhappy. Calls from his father before work always meant it would be a bad day.

"Is wearing my jacket over your bathrobe a new style statement?" he asked Molly on his way past. "And if you're leaving, I take it my lunch is waiting for me in the refrigerator?"

Molly's shoulders sagged and she held her forehead. She hated Monday mornings. "I never got to your lunch, Pete. I'm sorry."

His muffled snort told her what he thought of her memory.

She grabbed a loaf of cracked-wheat bread and slapped some ham and cheese between the slices, ignoring P.J.'s wails of distress.

"Mom! I can't be late!" he yelled.

"Another minute won't make that much difference," she said

as the plastic mustard container squirted water all over the bread.

"Pop," said Pete, "it's all settled. Remember? We agreed a month ago that I'd meet with Farmington Manufacturing and with Arleigh Fabricators to try to get their business. I've already met with Farmington successfully, and I'm meeting with Bud Carson from Arleigh today."

Molly tossed Pete's lunch into his briefcase. When he shut the lid, he would probably bruise the banana, but that was his problem.

"Pop, we can't change course midstream!" In spite of his starched collar and silk tie, Pete looked frayed. He closed his eyes in pain. "Pop, I'll talk to you at work, okay?"

He hung up and shook his head as if to clear it, looking a lot like Trojan, Mom's Newfoundland, when he came in from the rain. He turned to Molly. "I just remembered." He grinned at her apologetically, and Molly couldn't help grinning back. Even after twenty-one years of marriage, he still had the cutest smile in the world. "I don't need lunch. Bud Carson is taking me out or I'm taking him out or something. Anyway, no lunch."

He grabbed his briefcase with the lunch he didn't need and kissed Molly somewhere in the general area of her left eye. "Good-bye, love." She combed her hair with the fingers of one hand while she hugged him with the other. He climbed into his car and drove off without even a wave.

Do I have time to brush my teeth before P.J. pulls the doorknob off?

Sadly, she decided not.

"Mom," Amie shrieked, chasing Molly out the door, "my blouse!"

"Stop screeching, Amie. It isn't ladylike. Wear the pleats."

"But everyone's wearing bows!"

"Were you told to wear bows by Miss Hilbert? Don't clam up now. Were you?"

"Mom," yelled Jordan from the breakfast table, "there's no more milk."

"Too bad *he* can't sing," said P.J. "He's got the lungs of an opera star."

"Amie, as you go back inside to put on your pleated blouse, tell your brother to try the refrigerator," said Molly.

Without taking a step, Amie bellowed, "Try the refrigerator, nerd!"

"Okay, dork!" screamed Jordan.

Molly closed her eyes and pretended she didn't know either child. Then she walked to the car, and her stomach turned over.

P.J. was in the driver's seat.

"Mom! My blouse!" Amie yelled.

"Mom! There isn't any milk!" Jordan yelled.

"Mom! Come on!" P.J. yelled.

"I'm going to change my name," Molly muttered as she climbed into the car. "Then I won't have to answer any of you."

"Don't let us get to you," said P.J. He flipped into first gear and put his lead foot on the accelerator. "We just like to make you feel guilty."

"Well, you're succeeding. And, please, don't talk. Drive. Concentrate. Jerk like that when you go for your license and you'll fail the test. I should be so lucky."

"Relax. I'm a clever kid," said P.J. "I can drive and talk at the same time."

Molly moaned.

"Why are we taking you to school at this awful hour anyway?" she asked. "The janitor probably isn't even there yet."

"I have to work out with the weights. Mr. Davenport says I have a good chance of wrestling varsity if I apply myself. So I'm applying."

14

Wrestling varsity, another double-edged honor. What joy to watch one's sixteen-year-old first starve himself and then twist himself and some worthy opponent into grotesque knots.

"Does this mean you'll want to get to school early every day?" What an appalling thought.

"Nope. Only three or four days a week."

P.J. screeched to a halt before the high school. Tenth graders were supposed to feel awed by the privilege of attending, to be overwhelmed by the upperclassmen, and to proceed with all due caution until they'd tested the social waters. P.J. never considered such things.

He's not mine, thought Molly as she watched him stride up the walk. *I'm forty-four and I haven't a quarter of his confidence. There was a mix-up in the hospital nursery, and some other woman's got a shy, awkward, late-blooming boy who's really mine.*

She suddenly realized she couldn't slide across the front seat because of the gear console. She'd have to get out of the car and walk around. Glancing furtively to the right and left, she opened the door, then slid her feet, shod in their furry flipflops, gracefully to the ground. She hugged Pete's jacket to her chest and made a run for it, her pink robe fluttering beneath the navy jacket.

She was just reaching for the door handle when a deep and definitely masculine voice said, "Allow me, Mrs. Gregory."

"Mr. Davenport," she said. "How nice." She lowered her arm and stood daintily to the side as P.J.'s coach opened the door for her. She slid in.

"Marvelous boy you have, Mrs. G." said Mr. Davenport. "He's a real go-getter. If desire were all it took, he'd be state champion. Besides that, he's nice. Pleasant. Good standards." Mr. Davenport nodded approvingly. "All in all, a rare kid these days."

"Thank you." Molly smiled with genuine pleasure and hoped her teeth weren't fuzzy.

Mr. Davenport gallantly slammed the door, shutting six inches of flowing pink robe outside.

"Whoops! Sorry." He opened the door, and Molly reeled in her robe. The second try was successful.

As she drove home, Molly told herself she wasn't embarrassed. So what that Mr. Davenport was Superman, Cary Grant, and Tom Cruise all rolled into one. Charm was deceitful and beauty vain. She was worthy of praise, in spite of the headache that fretted her brow. She didn't believe herself for a minute.

Driving down her street, she passed P.J.'s and Amie's school bus and felt relief that her daughter was gone.

She glanced at her watch. In thirty minutes, Jordan's bus would come and she'd have six-and-a-half whole hours of quiet in which to build herself up for the evening's onslaught. How did working women do it?

Molly hung up Pete's jacket and went to the kitchen to survey the damage. On her way she collected four dirty glasses from the living room. Her nose told her to search further, and beneath the recliner she found a banana peel. She didn't even ponder how it had found its way there. Some mysteries of life were unsolvable and therefore unworthy of contemplation.

She had just put the peel into the garbage and the glasses in the dishwasher when Amie spoke from behind her. "If we leave now, I'll still be in time for rehearsal."

"Amie! You're on the bus!"

"No, I'm not."

"But I don't want to drive to school again!"

"Sure you do. Besides, you have to. Will you tie this bow? You do it better than me."

"Better than I," corrected Molly automatically. Her hands made a perfect square-knot bow while her mind kicked and screamed. "Where was the blouse?" she asked through clenched teeth.

"In the hamper," Amie said, patting her bow. "I ironed it." With such pride must Columbus have spoken of crossing the Atlantic. "Come on. Let's go!"

Molly sighed and got Pete's jacket out again. "I'll drive," said Amie. At eighteen she was an excellent driver, fastidious and cautious.

"No," said Molly, visions of Mr. Davenport dancing before her. "I'll drive."

Amie settled contentedly into the front seat beside Molly, chatting amiably. It pleased Molly to see how mature her daughter could be when she chose. It was as if the girl who lived in the Gregory house ceased to exist when she emerged into the real world. Manners, charm, and a sense of cooperation replaced the tempestuous Amie. It was a wonder the girl wasn't schizophrenic from the constant shifts.

"Thanks, Mom, you are a dear," said Amie as she climbed out of the car. "Now don't forget to hem my new slacks."

On the way home, Molly considered taking her hands from the wheel to knead her tense neck muscles. The car could drive itself home like Old Paint. It certainly knew the way well enough.

At the red light by the supermarket, Molly stared at a group of strikers walking in circles, their signs held high.

Unfair to workers.

No contract/no work.

On strike for better conditions.

We demand respect.

The blast of a horn forced Molly from her pensive study of the last sign, and she lurched forward with a jerk that would have made P.J. proud.

Jordan sailed out of the house just as Molly reached the door. She grabbed him and hugged him, kissing him noisily on his cheek, taking advantage of the propitious and all-too-rare opportunity.

Jordan pulled back quickly and self-consciously. "Hey, lady! That's no way for the maid to treat a son of the house."

Chapter

TWO

Molly sat at the kitchen table and told herself she wasn't depressed. But she knew she was. Every morning, every evening was a replay of this morning's chaos. And she was weary of it.

"I'm as bad as Rodney Dangerfield," she said aloud. "I don't get no respect, either."

She bit her lip so she wouldn't cry. The falling tears would only dilute her coffee and wrinkle the pages of her Bible. She read Proverbs 22:6 again.

"Train a child in the way he should go, and when he is old he will not turn from it."

"I'm doing that, aren't I?" she asked the big, gray cat named Mike Schmidt, who sat on the table staring at her. "And they're basically nice kids. So why do we always have anarchy and everybody ordering me around? I mean, who decided Mom was everybody's lackey? And why did they forget to tell me?"

In answer, Mike Schmidt came and sat on her Bible. He fixed his great golden eyes unblinkingly on her face.

"Oh, dear," said Molly. "You're hungry."

Mike Schmidt agreed, jumping gracefully down and walking to his empty dish.

On cue, The Cheshire Cat appeared, all orange with a white blaze, followed by the gray-and-black-striped Mazeltov.

Molly got up and opened the cat food as the animals wrapped themselves around her legs. Mazeltov leaped and tried to climb her back. Molly let him fall, a thud and an umph indicating that he had landed.

She walked to the cats' eating area in the corner of the laundry room while the trio banged into each other in their greed to be first.

"Sit!" Molly held the dishes high and a little behind their heads. With their eyes glued to the food, their hind quarters collapsed and they sat as though on cue.

"Speak. Say please," Molly commanded.

All three stared blankly for a moment, then Mike Schmidt tilted his great, furry head and bleated indignantly at the delay.

"Good boy," said Molly as she lowered the plates. "Too bad you can't hit home runs like your namesake used to. Then we could afford a real maid."

Still feeling forlorn, Molly wandered down the hall to the bedrooms. She looked in Amie's room first and almost gagged. Did all moms have to take Bonine to counteract the vertigo and nausea their daughters' rooms produced, or was she just lucky? How Amie had ever found her bowed blouse was beyond Molly. On second thought, if Amie had found it in the hamper, it may not have been such a difficult feat. The blouse had probably been the only thing in it.

How could someone so fastidious about her person be such a slob about her room? Did it mean a conflicted personality? Someone who couldn't decide whether she wanted to be a career woman or a bag lady?

Molly averted her eyes and closed the door.

The bathroom across the hall was worse. Wet towels littered the floor, the sink, and the toilet, with the end of one towel trailing gracefully, serenely, in the yellow water. Why there were five towels for only three children was another of life's unsolvable mysteries.

P.J.'s hair dryer and electric razor hung from one empty towel rack, and Amie's still-heating curling iron lay on the toilet tank where it rested against an empty tissue box. Jordan's dirty underwear lay under the edge of the vanity, and his Water Pic dangled, dripping on the toilet paper. The blotched sink proved conclusively that everyone had brushed their teeth.

The boys' bedroom was a study in contrasts. Black and white. Up and down. Bert and Ernie. P.J.'s bed was piled high with everything he owned. "It's cozy," he'd say as he adjusted his pile of *Campus Life* magazines to make room for his school books. Jordan kept the top of his bed—his unmade bed—clear of refuse. He stuffed everything under it: An encyclopedia—the R volume—the November Lands' End catalog, and his clarinet book. Three dirty socks sat beside a huge cardboard box of Legos he couldn't bring himself to part with. Various issues of *World, National Geographic,* and *Sports Illustrated* magazines made a teetering tower. Jordan's new birthday Bible lay splayed beneath a box of CDs and tapes.

P.J.'s Bible sat on his night table, and Molly knew even before she looked that she'd find the marker moved. The discipline that got him to school early to work in the weight room was the same discipline that enabled him to have devotions each morning while Jordan showered.

Mr. Davenport was right. P.J. was a great kid. So was Jordan in his junior high, caveman style. So was Amie with her beauty and gentleness.

So what's wrong, Lord?

Molly brushed tears away, but they kept coming. She wandered into her bedroom and stared blearily out the window. She sniffed so loudly that Mazeltov, indulging in his post-breakfast grooming on Molly's pillow, looked up, startled.

The bleak, early winter landscape matched her mood. The empty branches looked cold and hopeless. The dead brown leaves were torn, mere shadows of what they once had been. Even the sky was gray and sullen and depressing, as if it were ready to weep with her.

The phone rang.

Molly stared at it resentfully. She wanted no happy voice to greet her. She wanted to feel sorry for herself today, to believe she was doomed to wander unhappily forever, cursed by clutter and disrespect.

Suddenly she realized she had to grab the receiver before the next ring or the answering machine would kick in. She launched herself across the bed, just missing squashing Mazeltov, and grabbed.

"Molly, I'm running late!" said a distracted voice. "Do you mind if I don't get there to pick you up for thirty or forty minutes?"

"Sara!" Molly tried to remember where she was going with Sara. Bible study? No, that wasn't until Thursday. Shopping! The outlets! How could she have forgotten?

"Take your time." She looked in the mirror at her tattered hair, her puffy eyes, her bathrobe and nightgown. "I don't mind waiting."

Molly flew around the house, even getting her bed made and the kitchen cleaned up. As she watched out the window for Sara, she noted that the gray sky was slightly bluer and that the V of Canada geese flying south was honking happily. Maybe life wasn't so terrible after all.

The phone rang again.

"Molly, it's me."

"Hey, Mom. How are you today?"

"Not as happy as you apparently are," Janis Eberly said in a tone of voice that had all the charm of violins at a junior high concert.

Molly's stomach lurched, and her cheeriness withered like impatiens after a frost. "What can I do for you, Mom?"

"I just wanted to know if you're coming over today."

"Mom, I was just there yesterday. And the day before. Besides, you're coming here for dinner. Pete's picking you up on his way home. Remember?"

"Of course I remember," Janis said with all the delicacy of a woodpecker going after a rotten piece of wood. Not a cute little downy woodpecker with a discreet *tap-tap-tap,* but a huge Woody Woodpecker with a loud, penetrating *thonk-thonk.* Molly felt every peck right behind her left eye.

"I'm not senile," Janis continued. "I'm widowed. I just wanted to know if you were coming over today. We could clean the family room together."

Molly glanced at her own cluttered family room and shut her eyes. Resentment, guilt, and conscience resumed full-scale warfare in the pit of her stomach. She pressed a hand against her roiling abdomen and wondered how many antacid tablets she had left in the medicine cabinet. Undoubtedly not enough.

"We're going to that craft show tonight, Mom. We'll be spending the whole evening together." She smiled encouragingly into the phone. "I know you'll get lots of ideas for new things to make for your Christmas Cupboard."

Janis didn't respond, and a horror of a thought struck Molly, causing the hairs on her arm to stand at attention. "You are having your Christmas Cupboard, aren't you?"

Every year for as long as Molly could remember, Janis had spent the year making lovely handcrafted items which she sold the second weekend in December. She turned the first floor of her home into a shop, enlisting the whole family to carry furniture to the garage, set up display tables in the living room, and take personal decor items to the attic. On the weekend of the Cupboard, Molly and Amie served mulled cider and homemade sand tarts, wearing Christmasy dresses and gorgeous corsages that Molly's father always bought for them. The boys carried heavy packages to the customers' cars, and Pete directed traffic. Dad had always manned the cashbox while Janis mingled, laughing, accepting praise for her lovely work. It was pure Norman Rockwell, Eberly style.

"You are having your Christmas Cupboard?" Molly repeated. "Aren't you?"

There was a sad and drawn-out sigh. "I don't think so. I don't know that I'll ever do the Cupboard again."

"But, Mom! You've got a whole workshop full of beautiful things!"

"I just made them because I had to do something to fill my lonely hours." Again came the sigh, reaching its amorphous hand through the phone line to wrap itself tightly around Molly's heart.

I will not feel guilty about her lonely hours! At least not all of them.

She couldn't decide what hurt her most: her left eye with the woodpecker happily tapping in Morse code, her stomach swimming in enough acid to pickle it, or her heart wrenching in sympathy. Janis Eberly completely bewildered her. Molly had always seen her as the model woman. She was loving, intelligent, caring, strong, independent, outgoing, decisive, humorous. While these qualities made Janis feel no need for God, it would be hard to find a better parent—a better set of parents.

Then nine months ago, Ben Eberly had died suddenly while showering, and Janis's whole personality changed. She became indecisive, vacillating, critical, clutching. Molly didn't know how to talk to this new person.

"You must have your Christmas Cupboard," she wanted to yell at her mother. "Life must go on! You must go on! I need you to go on!"

But such a conversation deserved more than the telephone, and all she said was, "I'm sorry, Mom; I can't come over today. I'm going shopping with Sara."

"Oh?" said Janis, and that one word spoke volumes. Suddenly Molly was eight years old again, bringing home a note from school about her attention span. "Oh?" was all Janis had said then, too. But Molly had never allowed her mind to wander in class after that.

Feeling as much a failure now as on that day, Molly said, "Come with us, Mom. We'll have fun. We're going to the Vanity Fair outlet, and you can buy a new bathrobe. I'm going to get the warmest one I can find."

"Molly! Dad gave me my robe."

"I know. I remember. But that was five years ago, Mom. It's definitely showing its age."

There was a silence, and Molly realized that what she had meant only as general commentary was being interpreted as thoughtless insensitivity.

"Come with us, Mom. You know as well as I do that Dad wouldn't mind if you bought a new robe."

Molly saw Janis sitting at the kitchen table shaking her head as clearly as if she were there with her.

"No, I couldn't possibly." Janis said. "It would hurt him."

"Mom, he's been dead for nine months." Molly's voice was soft.

"You think I don't know?" There were tears in Janis's voice. She sniffed mightily. "I'll be waiting for Pete." And she hung up the phone.

Molly hurried to the medicine chest and grabbed a handful of Gaviscon. She chewed them as fast as she could and swallowed a full glass of water to wash the antacid into her stomach as quickly as possible.

How could her mother have changed so? How could she have become such a clinger, a manipulator? And how had she, Molly, read her wrong all those years? *Dear God*, she prayed, as she had more than once in the months since her father's death, *I thought I was a fairly perceptive person. But apparently I have as much insight as a romantic who thought Charles and Di would live happily ever after.*

It was unnerving to realize that quiet Ben had been the center of their home, not her mother as she had always assumed. Now she realized Janis was just the visible and vocal one.

Dear Lord, tell me. Should I call her back? Should I go over there after all? But I was there yesterday for four hours and the day before, too. How in the world do we get her to stop feeling sorry for herself? How do we get her to live again?

A horn sounded outside, and with relief Molly hurried out to meet Sara. She put all thoughts of her mother and her children out of her mind, assuming what Pete called her Scarlett O'Hara mindset. She would think about them and their problems tomorrow.

The two women had a fine time in Reading. At the Vanity Fair outlet, Molly bought herself a rich green fleece robe that zipped up the front.

"I think P.J.'s coach will like this, don't you?"

"I imagine," said Sara, with one eyebrow raised. "Do you expect to be modeling it for him?"

"He saw my old mangy pink robe this morning. I'd like him to know I don't always look so tacky."

On the way home, Molly's worries flooded back, and she stared sadly out the window.

"Okay, Molly, give," said Sara finally. "What's wrong?"

Startled, Molly looked at her friend. "What makes you think anything's wrong?"

Sara laughed. "You should see your face."

Molly grinned ruefully. "It's Mom."

"Janis laying on the guilt again?"

"How did she get this way, Sara? I feel like she's some stranger strangling me."

"She's just lonely."

Molly nodded. "I know. And she should be. They'd been married for forty-six years, and they did everything together."

Molly looked out the window at the still-gray sky. "When we entered the cemetery the day we buried Dad, she put her head on my shoulder and said, 'I don't want to be a widow.' I felt so sad for her at that moment, and I still feel terrible. And I miss Dad, too. Sometimes I even dream about him—and I never dream."

"I've heard it can take as long as two years before people function well after the death of a mate. You know—two anniversaries, two birthdays, two Christmases."

"Two years." Molly sighed again. "I hope I make it."

"You will." Sara grinned. "You don't really have any choice, you know."

Molly nodded in acknowledgment of the truth. "I think I could deal with Mom better if the kids weren't driving me crazy. I just feel squished in the middle all the time."

"What's wrong with your beautiful kids?"

"I don't know."

"What do you mean?"

"Just what I said. Something's wrong, but I don't know what it is." Molly was silent for a moment, then said, "How do your kids treat you when no one's around?" Sara had four children, three in their teens and a six-year-old.

27

Sara shrugged. "Fine, I guess. I don't expect to get the plaudits I deserve until I'm old and gray, but they do all right."

"So why don't mine treat me right?" Molly said. "I know Pete and I haven't been Christians that long—only seven years. Not nearly as long as you and Sam. But even before we trusted Christ, we were Christian in our value system. And since our salvation we've tried to 'train them up' as best we can. We've read James Dobson and Chuck Swindoll and lots of other guys and tried to follow their advice, but, Sara, something's still wrong."

"Like what?" Sara asked.

"Well, Amie orders me around, and P.J. constantly demands I do for him, and this morning Jordan called me the maid."

Sara grinned with understanding. "I've heard all that before."

"You have?" Molly was relieved. "You mean I'm not the only one?"

"When you teach women's Bible studies like I do, you hear all kinds of things, believe me." Sara pulled up at a stop sign. "Let me ask you a couple of questions. First, do you love your kids?"

"Are you kidding? Of course!"

"Do they love you?"

Molly sat quietly. Finally she said, "I'm sure they'd say yes, of course, but I don't think they think about it one way or the other. I'm just sort of—there." She sniffed, awash in self-pity.

"Don't go getting all teary on me," said Sara. "Tell me, did you love your parents?"

"Very much," Molly said. "But I'd never have dared speak to them as my kids speak to me. My mom would have looked down her nose at me and said 'oh?'"

"So you loved your parents even though they were tough on you?"

Molly nodded.

"But you're easy on your kids and you're not certain they love you?"

Molly nodded again, trying to understand the inverse logic.

"How does respect enter into your thinking?" asked Sara.

After a pause, Molly said, "The kids respect Pete."

"Why? Is he a more consistent Christian than you are?"

"No." Molly was thoughtful. "Being consistent in front of the kids is very important to both of us. We're certainly not perfect, but we don't practice double standards, either."

"Then why do they respect him and not you?"

"Probably because they know he means business and follows through. He doesn't make loose threats or toothless ultimatums." Molly made a wry face. "It's only old gutless here who has that problem."

Sara grinned at Molly's expression. "Here's a hard question for you. Are you willing to let your kids get angry with you when you know you're right?"

Molly looked pained. "I hate conflict. It makes me nervous. It's always made me nervous. Even when I was a little kid, I'd do whatever anybody asked just so there'd be no conflict."

"Well, you're in the middle of it now, aren't you? No parent ever raised kids without conflict. It's a matter of whether you're the victim or the controller."

Molly looked at Sara. "I'm the victim."

Sara nodded in agreement. "Do you know Exodus 20:12 or Ephesians 6:2?"

Molly smiled to herself as she rooted in her pocketbook for her New Testament. It never failed; Sara had a verse for everything. She flipped to Ephesians.

"'Children, obey your parents in the Lord, for this is right.'"

Sara shook her head and her sunglasses slid down her nose. "That's verse one. Read two and three."

"'Honor your father and mother'—which is the first commandment with a promise—'that it may go well with you and that you may enjoy long life on the earth.'"

"What's that first word?" Sara asked.

"Honor. Honor your father and mother."

"Interesting word."

"Very interesting," Molly said. "Sort of like respect your father and mother, isn't it?"

Sara nodded. "You're fortunate, Molly, that Amie, P.J., and Jordan are basically good kids who want to please you and Pete. Some kids are such rebels that there's no longer anything a parent can really do by the time they reach the age of your older two—except pray."

"You're right," Molly said. "My kids are basically good. They've been especially nice to my mom, stopping to see her after school or going over to do the lawn and other chores for her, even spending the night sometimes so she won't have to be alone so much. And they haven't complained, either. They've genuinely wanted to help her."

"I've noticed how good they've been to her," said Sara. "I've even said to my kids, 'See that? Be that nice to me when I'm old, okay?'"

Molly suddenly felt hopeful. "Maybe they'll just outgrow this lack of respect. After all, they grew out of the terrible twos. Maybe they'll come to realize they're wrong all by themselves."

Sara laughed. "I don't think it's that simple. Look at it from this angle: if we don't teach our kids respect for us and our authority, learning respect for God and his authority can be very painful."

Molly nodded. "I understand what you're saying, and you're probably right."

"Probably?"

"Okay, definitely."

"Another question," said Sara. "What do your kids do for you?"

"Are you kidding? I do so much for them and still they demand more. It's Mom do this and Mom do that. I never seem to be able to meet all their needs." She heard the whine in her voice and was appalled.

"I didn't ask what you do for them. I know you do plenty, probably too much. I asked, 'What do your kids do for you?'"

Molly was startled. "Why should they do for me? I'm the parent."

Sara turned into Molly's drive and put the car in park. "They should do for you because you're all part of the same family. They should do for you because they need to learn responsibility. They should do for you so they learn to do for others and be there for others who will need them in the future."

"Oh." It sounded so obvious when Sara said it.

"You're not being selfish when you require honor and respect, Molly. You're being wise and obedient to the Word. You're helping to assure your kids of ordered and orderly lives."

Molly collected her packages and climbed out of the car. She stood looking down at Sara. "Well, at least I have a name for what's wrong between the kids and me. Honor." She snorted, and little tufts of condensate erupted from her nostrils. "Of course, I have no idea whatsoever what to do about it."

"Yet," said Sara. "You have no idea whatsoever yet."

"Yet," repeated Molly. "I have no idea whatsoever yet."

Chapter THREE

ordan came into the house, dropping his guitar on the floor just inside the door. After tossing his jacket on a chair, he disappeared down the hall toward his room.

Molly grabbed the jacket and hung it up along with her own. Then she lugged the guitar to Jordan's room. "You forgot this, guy."

She heard Jordan grunt his thanks as she turned and went to the kitchen to begin dinner. Late afternoon music lessons were a nuisance.

"Amie, you didn't peel the potatoes," said Molly, disappointed but not surprised.

"Sorry, Mom. I forgot." There was no remorse in the voice that floated down the hall from the girl's bedroom. "Oh, P.J. called."

Molly's hand froze around a potato with eyes that stared at her. "I knew nothing good could come from wrestling. What's happened to him?"

"Nothing. He just needs a ride."

"What happened to his usual ride?"

"I think he quit the team."

Molly grunted. Just her luck. "But I haven't got time to go get him. Grandmom's coming for dinner."

Pete would have to pick him up on his way home. But he couldn't. He had to pick up Janis, and she lived in the opposite direction. Molly chewed at the inside of her lip, waiting for inspiration—which was very slow in coming.

Amie stuck her head out of her room. "Want me to go get him?"

"Oh, honey, would you? That would be great!" Smiling and humming, Molly took back all the nasty things she'd been thinking about Amie all day and concentrated on peeling and quartering the potatoes. She covered them with water and put them aside to cook later. Then she reached into the refrigerator for milk to make the meat loaf, and found an empty carton on the top shelf.

She shook it hopefully, but it remained determinedly empty. She scanned the kitchen for another but found none. Why was it that full cartons were regularly left out on the counter to sour while empty ones were returned neatly to the refrigerator?

Making a disgusted noise, she squashed the empty container. Mike Schmidt raised his golden eyes in reprimand.

"If you want food tomorrow, don't be critical tonight," she told the cat. "Jordan!" she yelled.

"What?"

"I want you to run to the store."

"What?"

"I want—" Molly clamped her mouth shut. She'd learned to be shrill to be heard over the kids' stereo systems, and she knew she'd end up shouting the whole conversation if she didn't stop now. "Come here, please!"

Jordan appeared, clad in layered sweat suits. "What, Mom? I'm going biking."

Molly nodded. "Good. Then you can ride to McCormick's for a gallon of milk, okay?"

Jordan shook his head. "Can't. I'm going in the opposite direction."

"You're going someplace specific?"

"No. I've just got to get away. I feel jittery from being cooped up at school all day. And then there was the guitar lesson. I haven't had any free time yet today."

"Then get rid of your jitters by riding to McCormick's for the milk."

He shook his head. "I told you, I can't. I want to go in the other direction. Besides, how can I carry a gallon of milk on a bike?"

"You manage baseball gloves and bats or fishing gear—including poles. I'm certain you can handle milk. Just use your backpack."

"Let Amie do it."

"She went to get P.J."

"When she gets back."

"I need the milk now."

"She'll get it. She loves to drive."

"I asked you."

"Let her. She'll thank you for the chance to drive some more."

"Go to your room."

"She really will."

"Go to your room."

"You'll be making her happy instead of me sad."

"Go to your room!"

The boy blinked. "What?"

"Go to your room."

"What'd I do? I'm only trying to help!"

"No, you're not! Go to your room!"

35

"I have to go biking!"

"You have to go to your room!" Molly took a step toward him.

He scowled at her. "Geez, Mom. What in the world's gotten into you?"

"McCormick's or your room, Jordan. Pick."

Growling, he went to his room, slamming his door in protest.

Mazeltov, who had been sitting with Mike Schmidt during the conversation, turned his back on Molly, stuck his tail in the air, and stalked down the hall after Jordan. He pawed the bedroom door until Jordan opened it for him.

"Well, somebody loves me," the boy said loudly as he scooped up the cat and slammed the door again.

When the older two kids finally arrived home, Molly met them at the door.

"Amie, run to McCormick's for some milk, please. I need it for dinner."

"Why can't you go? I just got back. Or better yet, call Dad. He can get it on his way home."

Molly's fists clenched. "We are not having a debate. Go get it. Now."

Amie looked shocked at Molly's clipped, nasty tone, but she turned around and went.

P.J. grinned at Molly and kissed her on the cheek. "It's good to leave the tensions of the day behind when we return to our cozy, gentle, loving home, Mom."

"Don't be snide. It isn't becoming. What happened to your regular ride?"

"He quit the team."

"And there's no one else?"

P.J. hesitated, then said, "No."

"So you'll need a ride every night?"

He nodded. "Every night."

"Joy."

P.J. grinned again. "You could solve the whole problem by buying me a car."

"Don't you wish."

Finally Amie arrived with the milk, and Molly got the meat loaf into the oven, the potatoes on to boil, and the peas cooking. While everything was busy becoming edible, she hurried to straighten up the house. Stepping over P.J., who was lounging on the living room floor in front of the TV, she quickly made the place look good enough for her mother—if Janis chose not to look too closely.

Molly rushed to her bedroom to comb her hair and put on some lipstick. She studied herself in the mirror, trying to decide if aerobics was doing her any good. Were her slacks a bit looser around her waist and thighs?

Sadly she decided that, so far, fun—if you could call jumping up and down in a shape-revealing Lycra outfit fun—was the only obvious benefit of all that sweating. Certainly, though, albeit unseen, her heart was pumping evenly and well, a marvelously tuned machine propelling life through her veins. After all, the brochure about the class had promised.

On her way back to the kitchen, Molly stopped outside Jordan's room. KYW News Radio out of Philadelphia sounded clearly. Every other kid listened to rock music, but Jordan loved the news.

Molly put her hand on the knob. He'd probably been punished long enough. If he brought up the trash cans from the road, they'd be even. And, if she were polite, surely he'd regret his uncooperative attitude.

She knocked softly. There was no answer. She knocked again, a bit louder.

Frowning, she opened the door. "Jordan, why didn't you answer?"

But there was no Jordan. She stood still in the middle of the room, trying to figure out what was going on. Suddenly her eye caught what it had missed before. One window was raised and the storm sash was loose.

"Jordan!" she screamed, furious.

"Mom! What's wrong?" Amie and P.J. both came running.

"The kid's gone out the window!"

"What?" Amie began to laugh.

P.J. went to the window, pushed the storm sash aside, and looked out. He too was laughing.

"Don't laugh in front of me," Molly snarled. "If we'd bought the two-story colonial I wanted us to buy instead of this rancher your father wanted, this never would have happened."

Chapter FOUR

As Molly slid the meat loaf onto its platter and served up the parsleyed potatoes, she fluctuated between fury, frustration, and fear.

She was furious at all her kids for their cavalier attitudes toward her.

She was frustrated beyond belief at her inability to deal with them.

And she was fearful that she'd lost their respect forever.

Stifling a sigh and brushing away an angry tear, she called, "Come and get it."

Pete and Janis, who had been in the living room talking about Janis's financial situation, came in.

"Well, dear, dinner looks very nice," said Janis, wearing a brightly colored warm-up suit that made her look much younger than her sixty-eight years. "And good news. Pete assures me that I'm not going to go broke in the near future."

Molly looked at her mother, startled. "Of course you're not, Mom," she said. She thought of the wonderful house near the golf course her mom and dad had shared, of their brace of

Buicks, of their country club membership. "You know Dad left you well-off."

Janis shook her head. "I don't know, dear. The bills keep coming and coming. And the taxes! I never knew before how much money they take from you! I just don't know what to do about it all." She sighed. "Ben always did everything."

Again Molly had that strange feeling of disorientation she'd experienced at seeing Janis's inability to be an independent person. She'd always thought her mother was the money person. She was certainly the buyer, but apparently she had no concept of where the money came from and where it needed to go, beyond her projects.

Molly turned to Pete in dismay.

"Mom and I are going to look over her finances this weekend," Pete said. "I'll see how much is there, what Dad actually had set up for their future, what her monthly income is—all that stuff." He patted Janis on the shoulder and smiled at Molly. "Don't worry yourselves, ladies. Dad was a planner. I'm sure everything is fine."

The three took their seats at the table. Janis looked pointedly at the trio of empty places and said, "Aren't the kids coming?"

"I'm sure they'll be here as soon as they can," Molly hedged.

"Oh?" said Janis.

Molly sighed and left the table to go begging.

"Come on, Amie," she said at her daughter's door. "Grandmom's here, and she's wondering where you are. You can call your friend back later."

Amie put her hand over the mouthpiece. "You guys start. I'll be there in a couple of minutes." She smiled dreamily. "It's Paul."

Paul, the youth pastor, was twenty-three, single, handsome, with a smile to melt any fair damsel and a godly spirit to mesmerize the faintest parent. He was a fairy tale prince come true, and Amie and every other single girl in the church from thirteen to thirty dreamed of becoming Cinderella.

Knowing a lost cause when she saw one, Molly moved on to the boys' room.

"P.J." She knocked at the closed door. "Jordan?" She hoped he had returned from wherever he'd gone.

"Be there in a minute," P.J. answered. "You go on without us."

Jordan didn't speak, but as Molly plastered her ear to the door, she thought she heard the window being lowered and P.J. whisper, "You're crazy."

She went despondently to the table and took her seat, avoiding her mother's eye. She listened with half an ear as Pete said grace and then began to pass the food automatically.

"So, Pete," said Janis with the air of someone determined to be pleasant even if it killed her. "How's business?"

"Aurgh!" said Pete. It was a groan of pure frustration, and it grabbed Molly's wandering attention from her disobedient son and her possibly impoverished mother.

"That bad?" Janis said. "What's the trouble? Poor sales? Labor problems?"

Pete shook his head. "It's my father."

"Sherm?" Janis looked surprised. "What's wrong with Sherm? He's not ill, is he?"

"No, no. He's fine." Pete paused. "At least he's fine physically."

"Thank goodness," said Janis. "I always fear the worst nowadays. I mean, if it happened to Ben, it can happen to anyone."

"That's a happy thought, Mom," Molly said.

Janis shrugged. "It's a true one, dear. But what's wrong with Sherm if it's not his health, Pete?"

"Just some disagreements between us at work."

"At work?" Janis paused with a forkful of potatoes halfway to her mouth. "I thought he was retired."

"So did I." Pete looked weary. "I can hear him now. 'It's all yours, son. I may have made Gregory Electrical what it is today, but it's your responsibility to take it into the next century, my boy.' He even threw himself a great retirement dinner."

"I remember," said Janis. "Ben and I went. It was a week before Ben died."

"Sure looked official, didn't it?" said Pete.

Janis nodded. "He and Marvella went on some big cruise to celebrate, didn't they?"

"Mom had a wonderful time, but Pop hated it," Molly said. "Absolutely hated it. 'All you do is sit around and read, or walk around some island and shop!'"

Janis nodded. "That's about it, but isn't that the whole purpose? Different world, different schedule, different places? Not that I know from experience, you understand."

Uh-oh, thought Molly. *Here it comes.*

Janis sighed deeply. "Ben and I never made it on a cruise. We always wanted to, but we kept saying, 'When we're older and less active.' And look what that thinking's got me. No husband. No cruise. No money to go on one. You never know when tragedy will strike, you know. All of a sudden, *boom!* You're alone, like me. But then maybe it was all for the best." Another sigh. "Where would I be if we had spent all that money on frivolous things like cruises?"

Molly looked at her mother. *We're commiserating with Pete here, Mom. Stick with the program.* She was immediately stricken at her insensitivity to her grieving mother. She patted Janis's hand and smiled sadly.

"Pop didn't like the cruise because he didn't have anyone to boss around," said the normally equable Pete with more than a touch of bitterness. "The captain never asked him how to run the ship."

Janis was jarred back to the present problem.

Pete took several gulps of water. "Sorry," he said, sounding embarrassed by his outburst. "It's been a hard day."

"Didn't the meeting with Arleigh Fabricators go well?" Molly asked.

"It went very well. They're going to give us the contract to do all the electrical work on their huge new facility. Now if Pop doesn't take it into his head to call them and try to re-negotiate like he threatened to when I told him about the deal I'd worked out…"

Janis reached out and patted Pete's hand. "I'm sure Sherm knows what he's doing, dear. Ben thought very highly of him, and we all know that Ben was a good one for evaluating people."

Molly didn't remind her mother that Ben had disliked Pete and his entire family for the first five years they were married. "Too uppity" was his evaluation. He preferred old money, not "that tacky *nouveau riche* bunch with the loud furniture and black velvet pictures."

"The Gregorys don't have any black velvet pictures, and you know it," Molly had defended them.

Ben would shake his fine, patrician, all-the-way-back-to-the-Mayflower-or-so-he-liked-to-think head and snort.

Then Sherm had given Ben a good stock tip, and suddenly Sherm, and by extrapolation Pete, Marvella, and all the Gregorys were "fine fellows, salt of the earth." Things had been hunky-dory between the in-laws from that point on. It sure made holidays less tense.

P.J. and Jordan suddenly appeared at the dinner table, took their places, and began to eat.

"You're late," said Janis, who never permitted tardiness at her dinner table. "Why are you late?"

"Hey, Grandmom," said Jordan, smiling at her. "I'm so glad you came to see us. How come you didn't bring Trojan along?"

Successfully sidetracked, Janis answered, "I came in your dad's car, and I'd never put Trojan in anyone's car but mine."

"I'm thankful for the consideration," said Pete sincerely. "That monster slobbers over every window, including the windshield, if he can manage it. I don't know how you can see well enough to drive."

"I make him stay in the backseat," said Janis. "He obeys most of the time. But even if he never obeyed, he'd be worth the price of his food for the security he gives. No one wants to tangle with a Newfoundland."

"But he loves everybody, Grandmom," said Jordan.

"But everybody doesn't know that, and I'm not about to tell them," Janis answered.

"Mom." P.J. looked earnestly at Molly. "I hate to be picky, but this food's cold."

Molly was stung.

"P.J.," said Pete, coming to her rescue, "Everything was fine when it was served. I know, because Grandmom and I came to the table when we were called. I think you owe your mother an apology."

"Sorry, Mom," P.J. threw her way.

"Hey, Grandmom," Jordan asked, "how much will you pay me if I rake all your leaves?"

"How good are you?" Janis asked.

"Terrific," he answered. "The best there is."

In amazement, Molly watched Jordan the Innocent. The kid had *chutzpah*. And no conscience. He was acting as if climbing out the window in direct defiance of her orders was an everyday occurrence. No big deal. Just ignore the crime, and it'll go away. Mom will never know, or if she does, she'll never do anything about it.

Somehow I have to hold this child accountable, Molly thought. *He's twelve. With luck, he'll leave home in six years, but if I'm to survive that long, I have to take action now. Nip the problem in the bud, strike while the iron is hot, and all those other clichés*—which were all clichés because they were true.

Molly sighed. She had no idea what to do.

Yet.

Amie came to the table as Molly was forcing down her last bite of potato. It was amazingly hard to swallow around the lump in her throat.

"Amie, Grandmom and I have to leave for the craft show in about twenty minutes," Molly said. "Will you do the dishes for me, please?"

"Gosh, Mom, I'd really like to, but I have much too much homework."

Molly opened her mouth to protest, but the phone rang. Jordan answered.

"Hey, Amie, it's for you. St. Paul."

Amie stood, a huge smile on her lovely face. "Hang up as soon as I answer," she called, and ran to her room.

Jordan glued his ear to the receiver.

"Hang up, Jordan." Pete's voice was quiet, but Jordan knew an order when he heard one.

"What's Paul want with Amie this time?" Molly asked. "She was just talking with him."

No one answered.

Amie floated back to the table. "I'm supposed to meet Paul at McDonald's as soon as I can get there," she said. "Can I have the car keys?"

"You haven't eaten yet," said Janis, pointing to the still clean plate.

"I'll just get a burger there," Amie said.

"Why are you meeting Paul?" asked Pete.

"To plan for Saturday's social."

Pete nodded. "I see. Well, you can't go. If you've too much

homework to help your mother, you obviously have too much to meet Paul."

"Oh, I can get my homework done tomorrow in home-room," she said airily. "And Mom doesn't mind about the dishes, do you, Mom?" She smiled her most engaging smile.

Molly sat frozen, uncertain of what to do. Then, *bingo!* a thought came to her. "Why don't you call Paul and ask him to come here? That way you can do the dishes while you wait for him."

"Mother! Please! I can't invite Paul here!" Amie looked horrified.

"Whyever not?" Molly asked. "Are you ashamed of us or something?"

"People will think I'm chasing him!"

Molly couldn't help noticing that the girl didn't answer her question. Translating "people" as Suzy, Alyce, and Mary, Molly said, *"People* needn't know unless you tell them. Call him back and invite him here."

"Mom, I can't!" Desperation tinged Amie's voice. "Believe me, I can't! Tell Dad it's okay if I meet him."

Molly looked at Pete questioningly.

"No," he said.

Amie's face flushed. "Dad! Please don't do this! Don't treat me like a child!"

"Don't you think Paul's parents ever told him no when he was growing up?" Pete's rational tone completed Amie's collapse, and she started to cry.

"Mom, tell him it's okay if I go! He'll listen to you. I know he will."

"I don't think so," Molly said, looking at Pete's set face.

"Yes, he will! He always does!"

"He always listens to me? Are you sure we're talking about the same man?"

46

"Mom!" Amie's face was scarlet. "This is not funny! How can you make a joke? You're mocking me! You're ruining me! How dare you!" Amie fled, slamming her bedroom door behind her.

The silence at the table was deafening.

"Why is she so furious with me?" Molly finally asked, bewildered. She pointed at Pete. "You're the one who said she couldn't go."

Pete took her hands in his. "Boys, Janis, will you leave us alone for a few minutes?"

"But I'm not done," protested Jordan, stabbing a cold chunk of meat loaf.

"Yes, you are," said P.J., who was watching his father's face.

"Let's go look for a good rerun," suggested Janis, pushing back her chair. "Anything but the news. I'm depressed enough already. Did you know I might be going broke?" she said conversationally to P.J. as they walked into the living room. "Maybe I'll have to move in here and take over your room. You and Jordan can live in the cellar. We'll build you a room in the corner by the furnace where it's warm."

"Grandmom!" said Jordan. "Tell me you're kidding!"

When the drone of the TV sounded, Pete spoke. "Molly."

She looked up from the crack in the table she'd been studying.

"What are you going to do?" he asked.

"About what?" She pretended innocence.

"About Amie. She can't be allowed to speak to you that way."

"I know. But I hate confrontation! I'm a marshmallow!"

"You're sweet and you're gentle, and they're two of the reasons why I love you. But you can't continue to allow your daughter to behave so selfishly and so disrespectfully. She lied to you about her homework and was more than willing to take advantage of you."

He reached across the table and ran a finger softly over her cheek. "We've talked about this type of thing before."

Molly grabbed his hand and held it to her face, trying to draw strength from him. "I know. And it's not just Amie. Today Jordan climbed out of his window and went biking when I sent him to his room."

Pete's gaze was steady. "And what did you do about it?"

"Nothing."

"Nothing?"

"Yet," Molly added with what she hoped sounded like resolve.

"But you will do something?"

"I guess."

Pete shook his head. "Honey, if love were all it took to be a good mother, you'd be the best. Or maybe I should say, if feeling love were all it took. But love, real love, can't allow a daughter to be disrespectful or a son disobedient. You have to be strong with them, Molly, for their sakes."

"Can't you keep on disciplining them for me?" She looked at him beseechingly. "You're so good at it."

Pete shook his head again. "I've been doing that for much too long. Oh, I could easily rush down the hall and lecture Amie and ground her; she certainly deserves it. But I'm not going to, because she didn't sass me. And Jordan—he didn't disobey me. He disobeyed you. I could continue to handle him, but secondhand discipline isn't going to solve the basic problem."

He looked at her earnestly. "Honey, you've let the kids get away from you."

"'Honor your father and mother,'" Molly quoted.

"Exactly," Pete agreed. "So what are you going to do about it?"

"I have no idea." She felt desperate. "Yet."

Pete got up and walked around the table. He pulled her to her feet and held her close. He rested his cheek on her head and rocked her gently. Molly melted against him, eyes wet. Through thirty pounds, Loving Care, and insomnia that disturbed his sleep almost as much as it did hers, he had been steadfast. Her rock. She locked her arms behind his back and held fast.

"Sweetheart," he said, "you don't need all the answers this very minute. Think about it for a while. Pray about it. But you must do something."

Molly pulled back and looked at him sadly. "Oh, I hate it when you're right!"

Chapter
FIVE

"A mie, that's my sweater you're wearing!" Molly looked at her daughter in amazement as she came into the kitchen the next morning.

Janis and Molly had gone to the craft show the night before and had a good time. Or at least as good as either of them was capable of—Molly with the kids and their terrible attitudes on her mind, and Janis with her "newly rotten life" on hers. That was the phrase she used when Molly dropped her off afterward.

"You and Pete and the kids are the only things that make my newly rotten life worthwhile." And she'd sighed with a gusto that meant Molly had to go in for coffee whether she wanted to or not.

After wrestling with Trojan through his standard exuberant and highly affectionate greeting, she'd stayed and listened to Janis until well after midnight. If she wasn't depressed before, she certainly was when she left her mother and returned to her darkened home and her sleeping family. She finally fell asleep about three o'clock in the morning.

Needless to say, she was not in a good mood when she came face to face with the thieving Amie.

"I know it's your new sweater, Mom," said Amie as she sat down to breakfast. "But I knew you wouldn't mind. You're such a sweetheart. Where's my egg?"

"Cooking."

"Oh." She artfully threw her shining dark hair over her shoulder. "Well, hurry with it. I don't want to be late."

"Jordan," Molly said to her younger son, who was rummaging in the cabinet, "how's your conscience this morning?"

"What?" he said distractedly as he rearranged the entire cabinet according to the chaos theory of physics. Finally, he turned and said accusingly, "There's no wheat germ."

Molly walked to the cabinet, reached around the muddle of jars and extracted the one item neatly standing on the shelf: the wheat germ.

"Oh," he said.

"Thanks for your help, Mom," Molly coached as she flipped Amie's egg.

He grunted as milk splashed into his bowl and out the other side. Then he picked up the dripping dish and dribbled to the table.

As she mopped up after him, Molly asked, "Amie, what did you do about Paul?"

Amie smiled with the unfocused gaze of reminiscence. "He came over."

"Here?" Molly smiled. "How nice. I told you he wouldn't mind."

"I tried to call him to tell him I couldn't meet him at McDonald's, but he'd already left. After he got tired of waiting for me, he came here to see what was the matter." She sighed deeply. "He was actually worried about me. And he stayed two hours."

Molly smiled at her daughter's fatuous expression. Suddenly a light, rustling noise on the other side of the kitchen drew

Molly's attention, and she looked over to see P.J. quietly but thoroughly searching her pocketbook. She flew across the room and snatched it from him.

"P.J., what are you doing? Pocketbooks are private."

"I need fifty dollars for a wrestling jacket."

"I haven't got fifty dollars for a wrestling jacket. Go ask your father."

"I already did," he said under his breath.

"Speak up, P.J. Mumbling is unbecoming."

"I already did."

"And he said?" Molly's voice was ice.

"I had to earn the money."

She stared, aghast, at P.J., who at least had the grace to blush.

"Mom, my egg's burning," wailed Amie, watching helplessly as smoke rose from the stove ten feet from where she stood. "Save it!"

"Two sandwiches," Jordan ordered as he started for his room, leaving his empty dish and glass on the milk-mottled table. "Thick ones."

"But it's only fifty dollars," said P.J., hand still on his mother's wallet.

Mazeltov leaped at Molly's back. She grabbed him and threw him at the passing Jordan.

"That's it," she screamed. "I've had it! I quit! No more good old Mom to order around, to take advantage of. You're all on your own!"

"What'd I do?" asked Jordan as Molly stalked down the hall, slammed the bedroom door behind her, and threw herself across the bed.

"Trouble?" inquired Pete as he looked up from knotting his brown paisley tie.

"No more Mrs. Nice Guy, Pete. I've had it!" She punched her

pillow repeatedly for emphasis.

The bed sagged as Pete sat beside her. "Moll, don't you think—"

"Are you going to lecture me?" She put her hands over her ears. "I'm not listening. I don't want a lecture! But if I know you, you're going to lecture me anyway and you're going to be right."

"Are you through being petulant?"

Molly rolled over and scowled at him.

"Don't you think it would be better if you used your anger as a goad to action like Scripture suggests, rather than behaving like this?"

She stared at Pete, then stuck her tongue out at him. "I knew you'd be right."

He grinned. "Whatever you do, Molly, I'll back you."

He leaned down and kissed her.

"Your teeth are fuzzy," he said.

"I love you, too."

Molly stayed in her room until everyone left the house. Amazingly, no one went to school hungry, unclothed, or late for the bus.

She made herself an egg, a raisin English muffin, and coffee. While she waited for the toaster, she wondered why her children performed well for everyone but her. Mr. Davenport thought P.J. was marvelous; and he was, outside the house. Miss Hilbert thought Amie talented and dependable; and she was, outside the house. Jordan was clever and considerate—his teachers kept telling her so; and he was, outside the house.

With her Bible, a notebook, and *Strong's Exhaustive Concordance,* Molly sat down to eat. Three hours later, she rose, creaky and needing the bathroom.

When she came into the bedroom, her mind was reeling with verses and ideas, and she shared them with the cats as she shooed them off her bed and began to make it.

"Did you know mothers have done all kinds of things in Scripture, some good and some bad? Rebekah made a savory stew for Jacob to use in deceiving his father. Not a good Mom thing. In Judges, Micah's mother made him an idol with which to worship God. Can you believe it? 'Here, Son. Let Mama help you be an idolater.'

"On the other hand, in Proverbs 31, the king's mother taught her son what qualities make a good wife. And Eunice passed her faith on to Timothy."

Mike Schmidt listened attentively, but Mazeltov and The Cheshire Cat wandered off, clearly bored. Molly watched their retreating figures. "It's a good thing you're not planning on being mothers," she told them.

She sat on the edge of the bed, and Mike Schmidt climbed onto her lap.

"The thing that struck me," she told the gray cat as she absently scratched his chin, "is that children are supposed to be a joy. Psalm 127 says so. 'Blessed is the man whose quiver is full of them.' Well, I'm not happy about my kids."

The cat purred with abandon, and Molly grinned at him. "At least you're happy, aren't you?" In answer, he reached a paw to her hand and guided it to his ears. She continued the scratching and the lecture.

"Proverbs 29:15 says that a child who gets his own way brings shame to his mother. Well, I'm ashamed—of my own weakness for allowing them to dishonor me and of them for being too blind to see what they're doing."

Mike Schmidt purred ecstatically. Molly stood up abruptly, hugging him. He began to squirm, obviously hating the confinement. She put him on the bed, where he walked to a pillow and curled up to sleep.

She began cleaning the bathroom. She needed the physical

movement to combat the turmoil in her mind.

When a mother's teaching was referred to in Scripture, it was usually with the idea that children shouldn't forsake it.

"So what have I taught them that they shouldn't forsake?" she asked her reflection as she cleaned the bathroom mirror. "Or better yet, what *should* I be teaching them that they shouldn't forsake?"

A litany of "one another" verses that she'd memorized in Sara's Bible study last fall burst on her.

"Be devoted to one another in brotherly love; give preference to one another in honor."

"So then let us pursue the things which make for peace and the building up of one another."

"Wherefore, accept one another; just as Christ also accepted us to the glory of God."

"...through love serve one another."

"...and be subject to one another in the fear of Christ."

"...bearing with one another, and forgiving each other, whoever has a complaint against any one; just as the Lord forgave you, so also should you."

"Do not complain, brethren, against one another...."

She rinsed the last of the cleanser down the shower drain and then stepped in. As she washed her hair, she continued to ruminate.

She and Pete were the only ones "one anothering" around this house. The kids certainly weren't. Somehow she wasn't teaching them to live here at home by the principles they all said they believed. They had no respect for her or each other. The only one they honored around here was Pete.

Once Pete had told her, "It's not a sin to tell them no, honey. Or to make them do for themselves."

At the time, she had smiled and thought, *Just like a man. He doesn't realize mothers are different.*

But mothers shouldn't be different, she now realized. They should be godly. They shouldn't give their children occasion to sin, and that's what she was doing.

She wrapped a towel around her head and slipped on her new green robe, then sat on the bed.

"God, forgive me. I have sinned against my children and against you. I have done all the physically needful things for the kids—cooked, chauffeured, washed, ironed, cleaned up after them—but I've neglected to teach them honor, for me and for each other. I need ideas on how to correct this situation. I ask for your wisdom and your courage."

All day as she worked, she thought. When she went to the grocery store, she passed the strikers at the other supermarket again. She watched them parade in their circle, and she pondered. She wrote herself notes as she unpacked the groceries. She muttered under her breath as she cooked dinner. She didn't hear P.J.'s complaint about the ham loaf or Amie's grumbling about the Brussels sprouts. Rising from the table, she said, "Pete, may I see you alone?"

The conversation in the bedroom was mostly one-sided as Pete listened to her scheme.

Finally he said, "Are you willing to take the flak you'll get if you follow this plan?"

"Oh, I expect the kids to give me trouble."

Pete shook his head. "No, I mean the adults who will criticize you—the people at church who will call you and your actions ungodly."

"How will they know?" Molly was genuinely surprised.

"Do you think those three out there carping over who gets the biggest piece of cake will keep quiet concerning what's about to happen?"

"Oh." She thought for a moment. "But any parent ought to support us. Honor is vital."

"When have parents as a group ever agreed on anything? For that matter, when have Christians ever agreed on anything?"

Molly was silent, reconsidering her plan. "Isn't it a matter of principle and pattern, then? The principle is 'honor' and is universal, but the pattern is at our discretion and therefore individual."

"Oh, I agree with you," said Pete. "And I'll support you. But anything unusual or radical is bound to be called unscriptural."

"I can take it," said Molly confidently.

Pete smiled, his expression a mixture of skepticism and pride. "Then make it two weeks," he said.

"Really? I thought one week was extreme."

"If you're going to do such an outrageous thing, do it long enough to have the necessary effect."

Molly shrugged. "If you think so."

"I do." He nodded. "But wait a minute." He got a worried look on his face. "I won't be home the second weekend if you do two weeks."

"That's right," Molly said, trying to analyze quickly how that would affect her plan. "The men's retreat. You'll be gone from Friday evening to Sunday afternoon."

"Maybe you should wait?" Pete obviously didn't want to tell her she needed him around to make this thing work, but it was also obvious that he thought just that.

Well, she'd show him! "I don't want to wait. I want to go ahead with my plan. If I don't do something right away, I'm afraid I won't do anything. It's now or never. Strike while the iron is hot. There's no time like the present."

He smiled at her clichés. "You're sure?"

"I'm sure." Her stomach wasn't. Her moist palms weren't. Her dry mouth wasn't. But her mind was clear and calm. "I'm sure."

"Well, I'm proud of you!"

She smiled at his praise and gave him a hug. "Shall we go tell the troops?"

He grabbed her hand and pulled her back. "Let's pray together first."

Smiling seraphically, Molly rested against Pete as he asked God to bless her radical plan. What a special guy he was. They left the bedroom holding hands.

Pete went privately to each child.

"We're having a family counsel at 8:30. Be there."

"But my favorite show's on then," protested Jordan.

"I'm sorry, but it's not on tonight."

"But I've got homework like you wouldn't believe," said Amie, looking fatigued and worn. It might have worked if a still-talking voice hadn't given away the fact that she was trying to hide the phone receiver under her pillow.

"Then you need a little break," said her unsympathetic father. He raised his voice. "And hello, Alyce. Or Suzy. Or whoever."

"Okay, you guys," said Jordan when 8:30 rolled around. He flopped into the recliner. "Let's get this over with so I can get to the really important things I've got to do."

"You're a real charmer, you know that?" said P.J. "Do you work at being obnoxious, or does it come naturally?"

"I learned everything I know at the feet of my older brother," said Jordan, smirking. "Thank him for my wonderful manners."

Pete and Molly sat on the sofa and waited. Gradually the kids stopped grousing and grew quiet.

"I'm going to begin this family counsel by reading 1 Peter 3:8 and 9," Pete announced.

"Uh-oh," said P.J., turning to his brother and sister. "Whenever Dad reads Scripture, something big—and from our point of view, bad—is coming."

The three stared at Pete suspiciously as he read, "'Finally, all of you, live in harmony with one another; be sympathetic, love as brothers, be compassionate and humble. Do not repay evil with evil or insult with insult, but with blessing....'"

He looked from child to child. "We want the spirit of these verses to pervade our home, and in light of this wish, your mother has something to say that I'm sure you will all find interesting."

From the recliner where he slouched, Mazeltov in lap, legs tossed over one arm of the chair and his body's weight resting more on his waist than his spine, Jordan called, "Yay, Mom."

Molly cleared her throat and ordered her heart to stop its unruly palpitations.

"Amie, P.J., and Jordan, I have two things to say. First, I want to ask your forgiveness for being a lax mother." She paused and took a deep breath. "And secondly, I must tell you that due to lack of respect and because of constant harassment, the maid has quit."

Chapter SIX

There was a moment of silence while the children stared at Molly as if she were crazy. Then a great wave of sound washed over her.

"A lax mother? Whatever does that mean?" demanded Amie, apparently offended. "You're a wonderful mother. Everybody knows that."

"What maid?" asked Jordan of anyone who would look his way. He grabbed Pete's arm. "What maid?"

"We forgive you, Mom, but what for?" P.J. was clearly perplexed. "What'd you do?"

Molly raised a hand for silence. "Let me explain. Look up Ephesians 6:2, please, Jordan."

"I don't have a Bible," he said.

"Well, get one, punk," said P.J. unsympathetically.

Barely disturbing his slouch, Jordan reached toward Pete. "I'll just use Dad's." He leafed through the pages and finally, with great show, began to read. "'Honor your father and mother—which is the first commandment with a promise...'"

Molly looked from child to child and thought she had never

loved them more. "I have been very remiss in not demanding from you honor," she said. "I have allowed you three to order me about as if you were the adults and I were the child. I realize how very wrong I have been and how I have given you occasion to sin. I have allowed you to be selfish, to be critical, to be irresponsible. Here you are, almost adults, and I haven't yet taught you how to behave as proper adults should. Will you forgive me?"

P.J. looked at her through eyes narrowed in concentration. "We're selfish and you're wrong?"

"I'm wrong because I've allowed you to continue being selfish or mouthy or whatever."

"Of course," said Pete to P.J., "you realize you're wrong, too, in acting that way to begin with."

P.J. nodded thoughtfully.

"But you're not a lax mother," said Amie earnestly. "You do everything I tell you—I mean, I ask you."

Molly winced. "Good slip of the tongue, honey. Tell is the proper word."

"But, Mom," Jordan said, several decibels louder than necessary, "what maid?"

"The maid who was also the chauffeur, cook, and housekeeper," Molly said. "The maid you wouldn't let hug you the other morning."

"Oh," said Jordan dismissively. "You mean you. You shouldn't let me get you upset when I act like that. I'm just teasing you and having a little fun. Really."

Molly shrugged. "So you say now. But it got the maid thinking, and she got so hurt by the lack of honor shown her that she resigned." She smiled at her brood. "In two weeks we'll have another family counsel to see if we can talk her into reporting back to work. In the meantime…" She paused and patted Pete's hand. "I'll take care of Dad's things because he works hard all day, but the rest of you are on your own."

"What exactly do you mean by 'on our own'?" asked P.J. suspiciously.

"Just what it sounds like. You each care for yourself. Of course, as your mother, I will certainly continue to love you and pray for you daily."

"Thanks," said P.J., obviously not impressed.

"Sarcasm doesn't become you," Molly said as she sat back to let the implications of what she'd said sink in. She felt light and hopeful. The world hadn't ended with her pronouncement, nor had lightning struck her dead. And, most importantly, she had taken action.

The three kids sat silently, thinking. Then questions erupted like Old Faithful.

"Does this mean you're not driving us places anymore?" It was Jordan, sitting upright, Mazeltov forgotten. "Not even to school if we miss the bus?"

Molly nodded. "The chauffeur got tired of too many inconsiderate, last minute plans, as well as the constant criticism of her driving style."

"What about mornings at the weight room?" P.J. asked. "My wrestling career depends on things like that, you know."

"You'll have to find another ride," said Molly, wondering if she was killing her son's college scholarship possibilities. Certainly two weeks wouldn't cost them $80,000, would it?

"Does this mean you won't hem my new slacks?" asked Amie. "And how about the dress you promised to make me?"

"The seamstress got tired of being given five minutes to do thirty-minute jobs because people didn't ask until the last minute. It also breaks her heart to see the clothes she's spent hours making being used as rugs."

"Mom," said P.J., horror tinging his voice, "does this mean you're not cooking for us?"

"What?" yelled Amie. "You can't do that!"

"Moms have to cook," said Jordan, eyes wide in disbelief. "It says so in the Bible."

"It says in Proverbs 31 that an excellent wife looks well to the ways of her household." Molly looked grimly at her children. "Believe me, that's what I'm doing."

"Mom, you can't do this!" protested Amie again. "Dad, tell her she can't."

Pete shook his head. "I'm behind her completely. My only complaint is that she waited so long to act."

The weeping and wailing and gnashing of teeth continued for some time as new implications of their mother's action occurred to the kids.

"Clothes?" asked Amie. "I suppose the laundress has quit, too?"

Molly nodded. "She took umbrage at being yelled at when clothes under the bed, on the closet floor, or anywhere but in the hamper weren't washed. She also found having to launder any one item three times a week a bit much."

"You wear the same thing three times a week?" Jordan asked Amie in disbelief. "No way. I've seen your closet."

"There are some things I wear," Amie sniffed, "that you do not see."

"Ah," said Jordan. "Those things. But they're so little you should be able to wash them yourself."

"Right," said Amie. "Just like you could make your sandwiches yourself instead of harassing Mom. 'Two sandwiches, Mom. And make them thick. I think you're trying to starve me to death.'"

Jordan's lip curled. "Ha. Ha. Ha. Very funny." His voice became falsetto as he said, "'Mom, my egg's burning. Save it!'"

Molly looked at her arguing kids and shook her head in disbelief. "Hey! Haven't we gotten a little far afield?"

"Sorry," said Amie, who then reverted to a subject dear to her heart: her clothes. "I suppose the laundress won't fold, iron, or put away either?"

"You always were a smart girl," Molly said.

"Lunches?" asked P.J.

"You can bruise your own bananas and mash your own sandwiches."

"Our rooms?"

"Not on your life."

"The cats?"

"They're your pets."

"They're innocent bystanders," said Jordan, holding Mazeltov to him as if Molly had signed the animal's death warrant and only he could save its life.

Incredulity quickly gave way to whining and petulance as the kids realized their golden goose had flown, and they were going to have to work for a living.

"And just what are you going to do with all your free time?" asked Amie nastily. "Talk about selfish."

"I'm going to design those needlework kits like I've been dreaming of for years and then plot a marketing strategy. I'm going to visit some of the local consignment shops and see what's involved in having them carry my work." She couldn't help but sit up straighter. "I'm going to become an entrepreneur."

The kids all but snorted.

"You don't think I can do it?" Molly asked, offended at their lack of faith in her abilities. "Well, just you wait. I'll show you."

"Food!" yelled P.J. suddenly, sending all three cats dashing for cover. "What about food?"

"What about it?" Molly asked.

"Who buys it?"

"Whoever eats it."

She sat demurely through the eruption, and when the volcanoes finally quieted, she spoke.

"The cook got offended with everyone complaining about her poor menu choices and cooking abilities. She got tired of no one showing up to eat her efforts. She got tired of fickle tastebuds and rampant waste."

"But how will I get food?" Jordan sounded panicky. "I can't buy it! I don't have the money. I'll starve!"

"Mom and I talked about this," said Pete. "And I'll be glad to ease your trauma."

"You're going to shop for me? You're going to cook for me? Or tell her to?" Jordan looked hopeful.

Pete shook his head and Jordan deflated.

"Then what?" he asked plaintively.

"I'll give you money with which to shop."

"Hey, great!" Jordan brightened dramatically. "A hundred dollars a week would be fine."

"Mom and I divided the weekly budget by five since there are five of us. I will give you that sum every five days or three times before our next council. That'll give you more money than Mom normally has, but not a bundle by any means. Still, even considering your lack of experience, with careful shopping you should be able to survive."

"McDonald's," said Jordan. "Burger King. Wendy's. Boston Market."

Molly shook her head. "The money will never stretch if you're eating like that all the time," she said.

"Yeah," said P.J., as if he knew what he was talking about. "It's a well-known fact that it's cheaper to buy food at the grocery store. Besides, you can't go out for breakfast, lunch, and dinner."

"Sounds good to me," muttered Amie under her breath, and Molly spared a sympathetic thought for the poor man her daughter would someday marry.

"But if I've got to shop, how do I get to the store?" Jordan asked.

"Good question," Molly said. "How do you think?"

"Walk? I can't walk! We live too far from the store. I can't lug all that food all that distance!"

"Calm down, Jordan. You don't have to walk unless you want to. Look around."

"Amie!" Jordan yelled.

Amie looked long-suffering.

"Or me," said Pete. "I go uptown myself every so often."

"Tomorrow, Amie, when you go to the store, take me," said Jordan urgently. "If I have to wait for Dad to go to the store, I really will starve!"

"Any more questions for me?" Molly asked. A grim silence answered her. "Good. Then I suggest we call it a night. And you guys might get up a little earlier tomorrow. Lunches will need to be made."

Everyone nodded and began yawning.

"Can I have a bedtime snack, Mom?" asked Jordan as he reclaimed Mazeltov from the mantel where he'd fled.

"Sure," Molly said. "Why not?"

"How about a crushed-ice milkshake?"

"Sounds great," she agreed, but made no move to do anything about it.

"You've got to make your own, kid," said P.J.

Jordan looked dismayed. "Uh-uh, I don't. Do I, Mom?"

"The cook quit," Molly said gently, her stomach cramping. The first challenge to her plan would come from her baby. She forced herself to stay in her chair.

Jordan stared at her, then shrugged philosophically. "Pretzels and juice are fine, too."

"I almost gave in, Pete," Molly said as they were getting

ready for bed. She was sitting on their bed, biting her nails. "Can I do it? Can I hold out?"

Pete halted in his task of hanging up his slacks and removed the hanger from his mouth so he could talk.

"Honey, the kid adapted. They'll all adapt, and they'll learn a few lessons in the process. Besides, if you turn back now, you're well and truly whupped." He leaned over and nuzzled her neck. "You have no choice but to continue."

Once again, he was right. Once again, Molly reached for the antacid. But she didn't get to actually take any for quite some time.

Chapter SEVEN

I t wasn't until dinnertime the next evening that some of the ramifications and repercussions of Molly's plan became apparent.

At the usual hour, she and Pete sat down to lasagna, salad, and garlic bread.

"Good as always," said Pete around a forkful of pasta.

"I'm glad you feel that way," she said. "I'm not used to cooking for two, and there are lots of leftovers."

Pete laughed. "It's so quiet around here. Where are the kids? Some fast food place? I haven't seen them since I got home."

"Food shopping. They left more than two hours ago."

"Two hours?" He grinned. "What are they doing? Buying the store?"

In answer, the front door banged open and the trio lurched in, bags in hand.

"Do you have any idea how expensive it is to buy food?" P.J. demanded of his parents. "I only have enough stuff for a few days and I'm broke already!" He was clearly indignant.

Molly bit the inside of her mouth to keep any trace of a smile from showing.

"Call me when it's ready, Amie," said Jordan, depositing his armload and heading for his room.

"Wait one minute!" snapped Amie. "What makes you think I'm putting away your food and cooking for you?"

"You're the girl," he answered innocently. Molly held her breath for the explosion.

Eyes shooting flames, Amie took a menacing step toward her brother. "Of all the insufferable, sexist gall!"

"Just tell him he has to cook his own stuff, for heaven's sake," said P.J. placidly. "There's no need for such overdone theatrics."

"Butt out and take care of your own business," said Amie acidly.

"I already have," said P.J. as he slid his TV dinner in the microwave oven.

"How did you do that, P.J.?" asked Jordan.

"Do what?"

"Make your dinner."

P.J. looked at his brother. "Are you serious?"

"Don't look so surprised," said Jordan defensively. "I only ever made popcorn in there before. I never made a dinner." He looked at Molly, though he continued talking to P.J. "See, we used to have this really great cook at our house, and she made really great meals, but she quit."

Molly smiled sweetly around her mouthful of lasagna and kept chewing.

"It's a shame someone of your tender years has to learn the bitter truth, fella," said P.J., "but the fact is, you just can't trust anybody these days, especially cooks."

The brothers grinned at each other, delighted with their cleverness.

"So what do I do?" Jordan repeated.

"Well, first, why don't you turn the box over and read the directions."

"And then?"

Molly looked at Jordan to see if he was being contrary. This was the child who could build all kinds of electrical gadgets, make glorious Lego creations, and construct models of great delicacy. But clearly the kitchen and all related tasks flummoxed him.

"Then you *follow* the directions," said P.J. wearily.

Jordan began to read the directions. "It says to tear off the plastic wrap over the French fries."

"So?"

"So what if I tear too much? What if I don't tear enough? I don't want to ruin this thing. After all, I spent my own money on it."

"His money," said Pete softly and rolled his eyes. Molly grinned.

"Just stick it in and nuke it with mine, idiot," said P.J. "They designed these things with you in mind, so they're fool-proof. Get it?"

"Ha-ha," said Jordan as he tore way too much plastic loose. He added his dinner to P.J.'s and shut the door, a feat that tilted his meal, angling the peas downhill and ready to roll out of the over-large opening when they thawed.

"What a dope," said Amie. She opened the microwave door and tried to slide her dinner in, too.

"Too much, Amie," P.J. said, shaking his head. "You've got to wait."

Amie glared. "Of course I'm the one who has to wait," she said. "You guys always stick together."

"Hey," said Jordan, staring intently into the microwave. "The plastic on your dinner is swelling more than mine. I ruined mine, didn't I? I knew it. Now it won't work right. I tore off too much plastic. I broke my dinner and now I'll have to go hungry!"

"Whoa, big fella," said P.J., patting his brother on the head like the Lone Ranger patting Silver. "Get a grip. It'll be okay. Believe me."

"What's that noise?" asked Amie abruptly. She turned toward the laundry room. "What are the cats complaining about in there? What's wrong, Chessy? Oh, dear!"

"What?" asked P.J. and Jordan in unison, hurrying after their sister.

"They're hungry! They haven't been fed! Mom, how could you let them go hungry all day?" It was an accusation.

"I believe the cats fall under your jurisdiction," Molly said, not confessing that she'd given them handfuls of dry food all day to fend off starvation.

"Starving poor animals just to prove your point seems cruel." No one could be as scathing as Amie when she set her mouth to it.

"I suggest you watch your tone of voice, Amie," Molly said. "You're already in considerable trouble for Monday night's performance."

"What performance?"

"When you blew up about not meeting Paul."

"Oh, that," she said dismissively. "It all worked out fine."

"But you were still disrespectful and you lied, if not in actual words, certainly in intent. As punishment, I've decided to take away your phone privileges for the week." Molly's stomach was teeming with acid, the lasagna curdling uncomfortably, but she was determined. In for a penny, in for a pound—to pull out another cliché.

"What?" Amie blanched, aghast. "You can't take the phone away!"

"Yes, I can and I will. We'll be more than happy to take messages for you, but until next Wednesday, you will not use the phone. You will unplug your extension and bring it to me this evening."

Amie was outraged. "You have no right! It's my phone! They're my calls! You can't do this!"

I shouldn't have had the garlic bread, Molly thought as she clutched her convulsing midsection. *Oh, how I hate confrontations!*

"Amie," said Pete quietly. "When I was younger and dating, my father took me aside one day. 'Listen to the way the girl talks to her parents,' he said. 'That's the way she'll eventually treat her husband.' Based on your recent performance, I wouldn't wish you on any man right now."

"Daddy!" Amie was clearly hurt. "It's only natural to get upset sometimes."

"Natural is not godly," Pete said. "You owe your mother another apology."

"I'm sorry," she mumbled, and as she bent to pick up The Cheshire Cat who was complaining loudly, she muttered, "Geez, what next?"

Molly noticed that, in spite of all the talk, no one had made a move to feed the cats. Poor, furry babies. The next two weeks were going to be hard on them.

"Tough luck, Amie, losing your phone like that," said the smiling Jordan. He was clearly enjoying every minute of his sister's sorrow.

"Just a second, young man," Molly said. "Lest you get too jolly at Amie's expense, I want you to know that I know you went out your window Monday."

"P.J., you rat!"

"I didn't say a word," P.J. said.

"Then how...?"

"I, soft-headed marshmallow that I am, felt sorry for you,

shut in there all alone. I went to tell you that you could come out of your room early. Imagine my surprise when I found you were not there."

Molly felt again the incredulity and anger. "Needless to say, I was furious. Disrespect and direct disobedience, Jordan: two cardinal sins. You lose your bike for one week and your radio and the TV for two." She had to keep raising her voice to be heard over her son's deep moans.

"But how am I going to get places if you're not driving and I don't have my bike?" he finally said, hitting unerringly at the weakest part of Molly's plan. "I didn't choose to live out here in the country, you know."

"Good point," Molly said, looking at Pete for reassurance. He nodded encouragement and smiled. The garlic felt slightly less lethal. "Why don't we wait until the chauffeur reports back to work—assuming she will—before you lose your bike? But the TV and radio begin now."

"What'll I do with myself?" No one could look as forlorn as Jordan when he put his mind to it.

"Read," Molly said, steeling her heart.

"Read?"

"Read," she repeated as the phone rang.

P.J., who was standing nearest to it, picked it up, and then said, "Just a minute." He covered the mouthpiece with his hand and looked at his mother. "It's for Amie."

The girl held out her hand, caught Molly's raised eyebrow, and slowly withdrew. Silently P.J. handed Molly the phone.

"Yes, Paul. How are you?"

At the mention of Paul's name, Amie let out an anguished groan.

"Amie can't come to the phone right now," Molly said. "May I take a message for her? Certainly I'll tell her. You have a good evening, too. Bye."

74

"Paul," whispered Amie as Molly hung up. She made a soft, keening sound. "I can't believe you wouldn't let me talk to Paul!"

"He said to tell you that Mary, Suzy, and Alyce will be at the meeting tomorrow night to help you finish your plans for Saturday night's party. The meeting will be at Mary's."

"Mary, Suzy, and Alyce? But the committee's supposed to be just Paul and me. Oh, I can't stand it!"

Amie fled to her room as the microwave buzzer sounded.

"Dinner," said P.J. as he slid his tray out. Jordan retrieved his, taking a little longer as he tried to capture his wandering peas. Molly watched absently as P.J., grinning wickedly, pushed a few buttons and slid Amie's tray into the oven. Jordan, smiling back, hit the on button.

The boys sat down at the table with Pete and Molly and seemed to enjoy their dinners in spite of having to jump up several times for silverware, beverages, glasses, and napkins. Whatever aberration caused them to use the latter, Molly was delighted to see it.

Jordan pointed at her with his fork. "I told all the guys about what you did."

"What did they say?" Molly asked.

"They said I should run away."

"And what did you say?"

"I said I'd think about it."

Molly forced herself to laugh along with Pete and P.J.

"How about your friends?" she asked P.J.

"Half of them said their mothers don't do anything for them anyway, and the other half said they wouldn't take such treatment from anybody, especially their mothers."

"And you said?"

"I said there was a chance you were right."

At his words, Molly felt pleasure flow through her, and for

the first time since the kids came home, she thought the lasagna and garlic bread might coexist peacefully after all.

"My secretary wants written instructions so she can try the same thing with her kids," Pete said. "She said she needs the rest."

"You told her I wasn't doing this for a rest, didn't you?" asked Molly. "You told her I was just using the same pattern God did when he withheld rain and peace and stuff from the Israelites to remind them to honor him, right? I don't want her or anyone thinking I'm doing this just to get a vacation."

"I explained it to her several times. Of course, I'm not certain she heard me."

"Oh, dear. Doesn't it bother you that she doesn't understand? Or am I just too concerned about what people think of us?"

Pete shrugged. "I knew people wouldn't understand. Remember I warned you? We just have to hang onto the knowledge that we know what we're doing and why."

"And we'll still tell people you're nice," said Jordan magnanimously. "Strange, but nice."

"If they ask," put in P.J.

"Thanks," Molly said as she stood to clear away Pete's and her dinner things. "I think I may need the endorsement."

"I'm just waiting to see what Grandmom says," said Jordan. "I'm her favorite, you know. When she hears what you're doing to me, she'll look at you and go, 'Oh?'"

Molly stared at him, stunned. "You know about 'oh?'"

"Oh, sure," he said. "In fact, we practice it, don't we, P.J.?"

P.J. nodded. "We've just never had the perfect opportunity to try it on you yet. Besides, neither of us can raise one eyebrow like Grandmom does." He proceeded to push his left eyebrow in an exaggerated arch with his index finger. He removed the finger, and the eyebrow settled to its normal shape.

"Watch me," said Jordan. "No hands." He raised his left

brow, but his right followed along no matter how hard he tried to prevent it.

"You look like Amie when she's doing her wide-eyed please-let-me-do-that-Dad-I'm-a-good-kid act," said P.J.

Jordan quickly brought his brows low. "That bad?"

P.J. nodded. "That bad. And what, by the way, my dear, sweet, little brother, makes you think you're Grandmom's favorite?"

"I'm the baby, and I'm nicer to her."

"Hah!"

Molly went to the sink. "Did anyone buy ice cream? It's sitting here melting all over the counter."

"Jordan!" yelled P.J.

"Don't raise your voice at me," he said. "I'm right here. And it wasn't in my bag."

"Oh?" P.J. said in a perfect imitation of Janis, and both boys practically rolled on the floor laughing. The ice cream continued to melt.

"Molly," said Pete as Amie reappeared, pale but composed, "is something burning?"

"My dinner!" wailed Amie as she ran to the microwave. She pulled her dinner out and surveyed the scorched, leathery remains. She glared suspiciously at her brothers, who smiled benignly back at her.

Apparently convinced of their innocence, she turned to Molly. "Did you have to do this to me?"

"Me?" Molly blinked, astonished.

"Isn't taking away the phone enough?" The girl looked as if she were going to cry.

"Amie," Molly said defensively. "If I were the cook, which I'm not, but if I were, you know I'd never ruin your dinner."

"Why not?" Amie asked, her voice exhausted from the emotion of it all. "You've ruined my life."

Molly glared at P.J. and Jordan, who suddenly dived under the table, crooning to and stroking their respective cats. But, Molly noted sourly, the boys were still not animal activists enough to feed the creatures. And their unrepentant grins flashed in delight at themselves.

"This is only day one," said Amie plaintively to no one. "I'll never survive two weeks."

Chapter EIGHT

The phone rang before Molly had time to feel too sorry for Amie, and she snatched it, beating Amie's automatic grab by a millimeter.

Janis's abrupt "Molly!" thundered in her ear.

"Mom," she said weakly but bravely. "How are you tonight, Mom?"

P.J. and Jordan exchanged glances and wiggled their eyebrows.

The boys laughed heartily, and Molly felt herself smile in spite of the agitation sparked by Janis's tone of voice. Catching herself, she clamped her lips firmly together. Her mother didn't deal well with laughter these days.

"What's this I hear about you quitting as a mother?" Janis demanded without preamble. "Just what do you think you're doing to my grandchildren?"

"Nothing, Mom," managed Molly, the urge to smile totally erased. How in the world had Janis heard about the strike so fast? However it had happened, Molly should have foreseen her mother's reaction. After all, her grandkids were her pride and joy. Why hadn't she planned for this possibility? Why hadn't

Pete? She shot him a help-me! look, but he was too busy eating dessert to notice.

As she felt her alarm spread madly from synapse to synapse, she felt like one of those animated, scientific cartoons where the little electrical currents leap boldly about the body. If she looked down at herself, she knew she'd see the lightning zigzags in bright red to signal panic.

"Nothing? You're doing nothing?" Disbelief filled Janis's voice. "That's not what I heard!"

"Nothing," Molly repeated in a barely audible whisper. "Well, not really nothing. Something, I guess. I'm—" She swallowed involuntarily, cleared her throat, and forged valiantly on. "I'm on a work stoppage until the kids learn to honor me."

"That's just what my friends told me, but I wouldn't believe it." Janis was incredulous. "Not my Molly, I told them. She loves her kids. She adores them. She'd never do anything so cruel. And here you are, making a liar out of me. I am so disappointed in you!"

"Mom," said Molly, desperation tingeing her voice. She fervently wished something would happen to distract her family, now all staring at her. Pete and P.J. looked sympathetic, Amie and Jordan gleeful. "It's not that big a deal, Mom. Really. It's not."

"Oh?" said Janis, unconvinced. Molly paled at the time-honored barb.

P.J. and Jordan looked at each other knowingly.

"Oh?" the boys said in unison.

"Oh?" said Amie, not to be left out.

"Oh?" said Pete, and the kids all looked at him in delighted surprise.

"He's got the eyebrow!" shrieked Amie. "Dad's got the eyebrow!"

Serious giggles erupted and quickly became full-fledged

laughter. Molly felt her lips begin to twitch despite her distress—or maybe because of it. She slapped her hand over her mouth.

"What is going on over there?" demanded Janis, each word clipped. She sounded remarkably like she had the day Molly and two eight-year-old friends had had a pillow fight in her bedroom and torn the down-filled pillow which had wondrously snowed feathers all over. At least, it had seemed wondrous to the girls until Janis found them.

"They're just laughing," said Molly, her voice quivering with the effort not to laugh, too.

"About what, I'd like to know?" said Janis, as imperious as she'd ever been. "Here I am trying to have a serious conversation with my wayward daughter about her questionable behavior, and all I hear is laughter. I repeat, what is going on at your house?"

"Uh," said Molly brilliantly, searching wildly for an answer that wasn't a lie.

Jordan smiled sweetly at Molly. "Not 'uh,' Mom," he said cheekily. "Oh?"

This time Molly couldn't restrain her laughter, though she made a heroic attempt. As a result she snorted directly into the phone—and Janis's ear—which made her cough like a consumptive, which made the kids laugh uncontrollably, which made her snort again, which perpetuated the cycle. She was wiping tears from her eyes when she realized she was holding a dead phone.

"Oh, dear." She replaced the receiver and sank to her seat at the table. "Mom's upset. She hung up on me."

"Because we laughed?" asked Jordan, radiating goodwill and love for all.

"Because I've gone on strike. Because I made her feel foolish in front of her friends. Because you laughed. Because I laughed.

Because I couldn't tell her why. Because life's awful for her right now."

"Other than that, Mrs. Lincoln," said P.J., "how did you enjoy the play?"

"Exactly," said Molly. "By the way, Amie, there's peanut butter and jelly in the lower cupboard."

"I think I'll have a grilled cheese," Amie said. "Or a BLT."

"Fine," Molly said. "Did you buy cheese or bacon?"

With a sigh, Amie bent and opened the lower cabinet, pulling out the peanut butter and jelly.

"Hey, Mom," asked P.J., "how did your first day as a designer and businesswoman go? Did you make anything yet? Do you feel like an entrepreneur yet?"

"It's not quite that simple," Molly said, feeling very professional being referred to as a businesswoman and entrepreneur. "But I do have an absolutely wonderful design I'm working on."

"Yeah?" asked P.J. encouragingly.

"You really want to hear about it?"

"Sure," he said.

"Well, you know that Grandmom and I went to a craft show the other night."

P.J. nodded.

"I saw an old-fashioned sampler there, a real antique from the turn of the century. It read 'Praise God from whom all blessings flow.'"

"The Doxology," P.J. said.

Molly nodded. "It was actually stitched on black paper in various types of script, and there were flowers and curlicues entwined around the words. I'd like to do a modern adaptation using the same words. Maybe on black cloth. I'm not sure yet. I need to try—"

"Sounds like a fine start," P.J. interrupted as he rose and carried his dinner remains to the kitchen counter, where he abandoned them. He sounded for all the world like his father used to when he encouraged a child in a job the child didn't want to do. "Keep up the good work, Mom."

Molly watched him leave the room, bemused. "I guess I should be grateful he even remembered I wanted to work on something. I can't expect deep, abiding interest."

Pete took her hand as Jordan and Amie followed P.J. "I was proud of you tonight," he said. "You did a good job. Now comes the real test."

"What?" she asked.

He waved toward the kitchen, and Molly almost choked. Amie's peanut butter and jelly jars stood on the counter with the knife embedded in the peanut butter. The open loaf of bread sat dehydrating between the jelly and the melting ice cream, now seeping out of the crevices of the container into a sickly brown puddle. P.J.'s plastic dinner tray sat beside his unwashed silverware and glass near the sink, his napkin crushed into the glass, his chicken bones picked clean. Jordan's dinner refuse filled the sink.

The still unfed Mazeltov and Mike Schmidt cruised the countertops while The Cheshire Cat sat on the floor, eyes raised hopefully to the others. When Mazeltov began to lick the peanut butter and Mike Schmidt grabbed a chicken bone, Pete shooed them to the floor.

"I can feed them, can't I?" he asked. "If I don't tell the kids?"

"Pete," Molly said as he opened the cat food can as quietly as possible lest the kids hear. "I've got to go to Mom's."

"Um," he said, concentrating on dividing the food evenly into the three dishes.

"Tonight. Now."

He glanced over at her. "Now? But we're already going to her place this weekend for the financial review. Can't it wait? And get down, you wayward beast." He swung at Mike

83

Schmidt, who was once again sitting on the counter, drooling unbecomingly.

"Now. She was really upset. I could tell. I mean, she hung up on me. My mom! On me!"

Pete tiptoed to the laundry room and set the cat food carefully on the floor. Then he came back to the kitchen and washed the fish smell from his hands. "Well, Janis wanted me to look at a couple of dripping faucets for her. I'll come along to protect your good name."

Molly wrapped her arms around her husband and laid her head on his chest. "You are a good man."

"I'm glad you think so." He kissed the top of her head. "It seems nowadays that all we've got is each other."

Molly stepped back and looked at Pete. There was a note in his voice she rarely heard. "What's wrong? This strike business isn't getting you down, is it? It's something else; it's got to be."

He drew a deep, ragged breath. "Pop is driving me nuts!" He walked to the closet and pulled his jacket from its hanger, then shoved his arms into the sleeves.

They were well on their way to Janis's house before Molly returned to the topic of Sherm.

"What happened today, Pete?" she asked. "What did Pop do now?"

Pete glanced at her, and she saw in the glow of the streetlight that his face showed a troubled confusion, probably the same expression she wore when she talked about Janis.

"He accused me of wanting to bankrupt Gregory Electrical. All I want to do is bleed the company of its assets and sell out, abandoning the employees he's nurtured with such care. My goal is to destroy all he's built the last forty years. I'm an ingrate and a lousy businessman, and how can I do this to him? Where's my respect?"

"Pete! But you two always worked together so well!"

84

"Because I did everything his way," Pete said grumpily. "But his way is old hat now, Molly. It really is. We've been existing on momentum for several years now. If things don't change, we're going to find ourselves sliding backwards while more and more new guys zoom past us."

"But Pop was always such a good businessman, a successful businessman."

Pete nodded. "He was. In his time he was very innovative and creative. But now he's too rich and content. He's been too successful doing things his way. But we need to do new things in new ways."

"Aren't you the boss now?"

"Sure. At least legally. But what do I do when he countermands all my orders? I spent months planning the presentation to Arleigh Fabricators, and we made a wonderful impression."

Molly nodded. "I remember. You got the contract for all their electrical needs for their big new plant."

Pete was silent.

"Didn't you?" asked Molly.

"I thought so. They said so. But then Pop read the paperwork, didn't like what he saw, and called them to reopen negotiations. Without telling me." Frustration frayed Pete's voice.

"Can he do that?"

"Of course not. But what do I do? Sic the lawyers on my own father?"

"Well," said Molly, flailing wildly for something comforting to say, "maybe they'll just ignore him."

Pete snorted and Molly had to admit that Sherm Gregory was not a man people ignored. He'd never let them.

"Gus Carson called this morning and asked me who was in charge at Gregory Electrical. 'If it's the old man,' he said, 'count me out. And if it's not, you'd better convince me of who it is if you want my business. I don't have time for your family spats. I have more than enough troubles of my own!'"

"Oh, Pete!" Molly stared helplessly at her husband. She thought of all the years he'd been the good son, the willing and cooperative lieutenant.

"Here's a little example of what it's like," Pete said. "I asked Marge, the office manager, to get me some more paper clips. I asked her to get the plastic coated ones, big and small, because I like them. Pop saw the boxes sitting on my desk, yelled at Marge, and made her send them back. 'But Pete asked for this kind,' she said. 'He did not,' Pop said. 'He knows we always use the metal kind.'"

"I bet Marge wasn't too happy," Molly said. "She can be touchy even in the best of times."

"When I said something to Pop, he got very defensive. He said I have no appreciation of all the years he slaved over this company just so he could pass it on to me. I have no idea of what it cost him to build the company. I have no concept of the time, energy, and sweat he poured into it, and he didn't do it so I could run it into the ground! By Jove, he did not! 'And you call yourself a Christian!' he yelled at me when he was leaving. 'Hah!'"

"He didn't!" Molly was appalled. "I know he and your mom find our becoming Christians a bit strange, but they've never said anything so hurtful before."

"It just shows how upset he is."

"But it's so unfair!"

Pete turned into Janis's drive. "Let's not talk about it any-more. My head's pounding as it is. I just want to go in here and fix a dripping faucet for my appreciative mother-in-law," he said. "I want to remind myself that I can do something right after all."

Well, look who's here," said Janis as she opened the door. She was wearing the ratty old bathrobe her husband had given her. Trojan pranced madly beside her, his barks shaking the storm door.

"Shut up, dog!" Janis hissed to the beast, who ignored her completely. He butted by her and jumped up, putting his feet affectionately on Molly's shoulders. As she staggered under the burden of his love, she heard her mother say coolly, "To what do I owe the pleasure?"

"Mom, you hung up on me," Molly said as Pete took Trojan by the collar and pulled him back down to earth. Trojan cooperatively turned his great, shaggy black head and his affectionate welcome on Pete.

Molly couldn't help but notice that not only was Janis's tone of voice anything but welcoming, she hadn't moved aside to let them enter.

"You laughed at me!" There was genuine hurt in Janis's voice.

"I did not," Molly said. "I'd never laugh at you. I was laughing at the kids."

"And what were they doing that was so funny? I would have thought that they wouldn't be laughing about anything, the way you're treating them."

"Molly's not doing anything that harms the kids, Mom," Pete said, leaning across Trojan to kiss Janis on the cheek. "And I came over to fix your dripping faucets, not to stand on your doorstep."

"You're too good for her, Pete," Janis said, turning and walking into the living room where the TV blared a tabloid news show. "A charming, handsome man like you saddled with a woman like her. Sad. So very sad."

"I seem to remember a time when you felt it was the other way around," Pete said with a smile as he dropped his coat on the sofa.

"Hang your coat up," Janis ordered. "Why do you think I have closets? And a woman can change her mind, you know."

"Oh?" said Pete, eyebrow raised as he turned to hang up his coat.

The comment went right over Janis's head, but Molly had to rush into the powder room so she wouldn't laugh twice in one evening. Or maybe she would cry. She thought it could go either way. She took several deep breaths as she came to the conclusion that nerves and stress could do terrible things to a person's equanimity.

Trojan began scratching at the bathroom door, and Molly opened it to let him in. The little room suddenly became quite crowded as he pressed himself against her in adoration. She patted him absently as she stared at herself in the mirror, wondering where this woman who could laugh at her own mother—well, not really *at* her mother—had come from. Probably the same place the woman who let her kids fend for themselves came from.

The big question was: Was this new woman good or bad? A

godly woman or her evil twin?

"Ask me again in two weeks," she told Trojan, who proved his interest in her predicament by washing half her face in one great sweep of his very wet tongue.

She came out of the powder room mopping her face and found Pete and Janis in the kitchen.

"See?" Janis said, pointing at the kitchen sink and the drip, drip, drip.

"Let me get Dad's toolbox," Pete said, and started down the cellar stairs, a firm hand on the railing to keep from being dumped over the edge by the enthusiastic Trojan.

Janis and Molly stood uncertainly in the red-and-white kitchen, eyeing each other.

Finally Janis spoke. "You never did anything like this strike thing before."

Molly nodded. "I never had the courage."

"The courage? The insanity is more like it."

"Mom, they're basically good kids—"

"I should say they are!" interrupted Janis.

"—but they treat me very disrespectfully. I decided I wanted that behavior stopped."

"But something so extreme? Something people talk about?"

"What would you rather me do, Mom? Let them continue running all over me?"

"But there must be another way!"

"What? Yell at them? Oh, sure. I can hear me screaming, 'Jordan, don't you dare talk to me like that. I want you to apologize right now! Who do you think you are, young man, treating me that way?'" Molly looked at Janis with a wry smile. "Now that's really me."

Janis gave a half smile in response. "It does sound stupid to think of you yelling. You've never yelled at anyone your whole life."

"And even if I was a yeller, would that make it right? What kind of a home would that be?"

"A noisy one," said Pete as he set the toolbox on the kitchen table. "And, Mom, you need to know that I support Molly completely in what she's doing. The kids *are* too disrespectful of her. She needed to do something. I'm just glad she stopped being a pushover."

Janis patted Trojan absently as she watched Pete wrestle the end piece off the spigot and take out the defective washer, but it was obvious she was thinking about other things. Finally she turned to Molly.

"But somehow it doesn't seem Christian!" she said.

"Why?" Molly asked, fascinated that her mother, like Sherm, was bothered by this point. "What doesn't seem Christian about it?"

"Christians are supposed to be gentle and kind and nice," Janis said. "Like you've always been. That's why I was so surprised and skeptical when you said a few years ago that you were suddenly 'saved.' To me you'd always been the warm and loving person a Christian is supposed to be."

Molly was touched by her mother's words, and she threw her arms around Janis.

"Mom, what a nice thing to say!"

"Well, it's true," Janis mumbled into Molly's shoulder. "Isn't it, Pete?"

Pete laid down his wrench and wrapped his arms about both women as Trojan wiggled his way into the middle of the huddle. "You're right, Mom. She is a warm and wonderful woman. But there's a difference between being gentle and kind, and being a pushover."

"Besides," said Molly as she pulled back and sank into a kitchen chair, "being nice and gentle has nothing to do with becoming a Christian. That's got to do with believing in Jesus as your Savior. And afterwards, being a Christian has to do with living according to the Bible. And the Bible clearly says, 'Honor your father and mother.' All I'm trying to do is teach my kids the truth of that."

Pete reclaimed the wrench and asked, "What other faucets?"

"My bathroom sink and the shower in the main bathroom. Here, I'll show you."

Molly and Trojan followed the two upstairs and stood in the bathroom doorway as Janis and Pete discussed what was wrong with the shower head. When Trojan went forward to offer his suggestions, Molly turned quietly and went down the hall to the large room over the garage that was Janis's workroom. It was here that her mother created and stored the wonderful crafts, bouquets, and wreaths that drew hundreds of people to the Christmas Cupboard each year.

Molly stared at the closed door for a minute, disconcerted. It should be open, lights on, last-minute projects filling the work space, Christmas music blaring. Janis had the largest collection of Christmas music Molly had ever seen. To see the room closed and quiet was somehow scary.

Slowly she turned the knob and flicked on the light switch. She gasped and grabbed her heart.

The shelves that Ben had built for Janis's creations were almost empty, and this was the time of year when they should have been brimming with product and color and imagination, ribbons and sparkles and beauty.

And the work benches! They were littered with dozens of partially completed projects. Wreath frames with pine cones and flowers lying beside them. Angels with gowns but no wings or heads. Dried arrangements with flowers stuffed haphazardly in one side of the container. Miniature Christmas trees with only the top half decorated. Wall hangings that read MERR— or NOE— or JESUS IS THE REA—. Woolly sheep with half their wool missing. A large, disorderly pile of clothes-pins lay next to artificial greens, narrow red ribbon, and miniature pine cones.

And scattered among the aborted projects were dirty paint brushes, uncapped paints, unwound spools of wire, dried and silk flowers lying helter-skelter, and tools tossed everywhere.

"Always remember," a stern Janis had told the young Molly with frustrating frequency, "you must clean up after yourself without fail or you will lose things and waste valuable product and time. And never begin a new project until you've completed the old."

As she stared at the clutter, Molly felt her eyes fill with tears. She leaned against a counter for support.

"Oh, Mom," she whispered as she picked up a spool of wire and automatically began rewinding it. Nothing could have shown Janis's emotional state more clearly than this room did. Molly was broken by the pain it represented.

"Ah, Pete," Janis's voice echoed from the bathroom, "what would I do without you? Only one more left."

Quickly Molly turned off the light and pushed the door closed. She listened as her husband and mother walked past on their way to Janis's bathroom and leaking tap. She tensed as she heard Trojan snuffle at the bottom of the door, but relaxed when Janis called, "Get away from there, Trojan."

When they were all past, Molly cautiously opened the door. Seeing that the coast was clear, she rushed downstairs. She had to get control of herself before she faced her mother again.

The pain of her father's death hadn't been this sharp in months.

If I feel this bad, she thought, *what must it be like for Mom?* Christmas was a hard enough time for someone who was grieving, but with all the memories of the Christmas Cupboard...

And that room! Dad had designed it and remodeled it

expressly for her to work in. No one had been prouder of Janis's Christmas Cupboard than Ben.

"She's going to support me in my old age," he told everyone who praised her work. "I've got the names of all the arthritis specialists in the area in case she has the bad taste to get infirm. I can't count on Social Security, but I can count on Janis's creativity and talent."

Once a client had asked Janis why she didn't open a shop so that people could have the pleasure of buying her wonderful creations all year. Before she had a chance to answer, Ben slipped his arm around her shoulders and said, "I can't spare her that much. She's so good, I know she'd be a great success. And then I'd never see her. I don't know if I can deal with a loss that great."

Instead, it had been Janis who had had to deal with the loss.

Were there some things too hard to tough your way through? Molly thought about that as she heard Pete drop some tool above her head. Was it too much to ask of Janis that she have a Christmas Cupboard this year? Or maybe ever again?

But you have to fight on, or you might as well climb into bed and stay there until you die, too.

Molly was so lost in thought that Pete, Janis, and Trojan were in the room before she was even aware they had come downstairs.

"What are you doing, sitting here alone?" asked Janis.

"Watching TV," Molly said quickly, focusing to see what was on. Trojan came loping over and bumped her with his great head, begging her to scratch him around the ears. When she reached out, she saw that she still had the spool of wire in her hand. In what she hoped looked like a natural movement, she stuffed it in the waistband of her jeans, where it persisted in jabbing her painfully every time she moved.

The first thing she did when she was finally in the car was

pull the spool out and rub her sore stomach.

"Wire pricks," she explained to Pete, who was watching with interest. "It's from Mom's studio. And, Pete! Nothing's done! Nothing! She can't finish anything." She pulled a ratty tissue from her pocket and blew her nose. She was surprised to see that her hands were shaking a little. "How could we have been so blind as to not see?"

"Hey, Molly." Pete reached for her hand. "You've been aware. You've been very kind to her. We all have."

"But I didn't understand, Pete. I didn't realize how completely she has dried up inside."

They sat in silence, holding hands, and Molly wept.

Chapter TEN

Molly stared at herself in the mirror. She studied the circles under her eyes from the sleepless nights spent worrying about her mother. She grabbed a concealer stick and tried to diminish the damage, but makeup could only go so far. And her body, clad in a new Sears special, an emerald green leotard and tights, was something else again.

"An avocado with arms and legs. A fir tree with a cellulite trunk. A sweet gherkin. Disgusting."

She pulled on slacks and a shirt, grabbed her purse and Bible, and left the chaos behind. Her breakfast dish and coffee cup and Pete's cereal bowl and juice glass sat pristinely in the dishwasher. The rest of the breakfast dishes mingled with yesterday's debris in a pattern not even an artist of the most abstract school could have imagined.

One concession to neatness that Molly had made was to push the container of thoroughly melted ice cream, still lying on the counter, into the sink so its contents would seep down the drain instead of onto the floor. She also erected a dam with some paper towels to keep what had already melted from running down the front of the cabinets.

She really ought to mail a note to the ice cream manufacturers about the high quality of their container. The puddle this morning was barely larger than the puddle had been last night. Of course, the cats might have had something to do with that.

Aerobics class required enough concentration that the kids and Janis and Sherm all disappeared from her mind.

"Step to the side, fall back. Step, step, kick, ball change. Pivot turn, run-run, pivot turn, break, break," called the instructor, who was an impossibly lithe, slim, young thing named Ashley. She wore a mauve two-piece exercise outfit that made her look absolutely wonderful. Not an ounce of fat showed anywhere around her middle, her slim legs in their white tights went on forever, and her oh-so-chic blond hair even stayed in place as she bounced and moved. It was a good thing she was nice, or Molly would have had to dislike her on general principle.

Concentrating, moving in time to the music, stretching, panting, Molly enjoyed herself immensely. Maybe by the next class her calves wouldn't even hurt anymore.

"You're getting very adept, Mrs. Gregory," the gorgeous Ashley said as Molly walked around, gasping and taking her pulse between numbers.

As she puffed out, "That's because you're much better than any exercise tape," Molly noted morosely that Ashley's breathing rate wasn't even elevated. *Maybe someday,* she thought with a touch of envy.

After class, Molly slid back into her slacks and shirt and drove to Sara's for their weekly Bible study. She was pleased to note that by the time she rang the doorbell, her breathing had returned to normal.

"Molly," said Jodi Bartkowski as soon as Molly walked through the door, "tell me what's going on. Aaron brought home some cockamamie story about your being on strike.

Jordan told him you got mad and just walked off the job, and he hasn't any idea why."

"Oh, he knows, all right. Don't buy that line."

"Well, you ought to know that he asked if he could move in with us for a couple of weeks." Jodi smiled. "Not that I want him or any kid but my own for that long."

Molly snapped open a Diet Coke, grabbed a granulated sugar donut—so much neater in public than the powdered sugar ones—and took a seat.

"If you want to get technical, I'm not really on strike," said Molly around a swallow of her Coke. "I'm on a work stoppage."

"And there's a difference?" asked Jodi.

"Sure," said Molly. "A strike is when workers seek better conditions for themselves. I'm not looking for better conditions for me."

"You're not?" Jodi brushed the powdered sugar from her donut off her brown sweater while Molly looked complacently at her neat, granulated donut. "Then what are you looking for?"

"What's this about striking?" asked Daisy Johannsen, a young mother of two girls. She set her coffee cup down, and Molly noticed she had no donut. No wonder she stayed a size seven. "I didn't know you were working, let alone striking."

"Just working at home, Daisy, at the Molly Gregory Design Studio."

Now where had that name come from? But it sounded wonderful, so professional and businesslike. It ought to impress Daisy, who ran an editing business called Red Pencil Enterprises from her home and was always encouraging Molly to do more than "just" needlework.

"You need to find yourself, Molly, use your mind," she'd say ever so earnestly. "You're one smart lady. You just don't know it yet."

The fact that it was never "just" needlework to Molly any

more than it was "just" cooking to a chef never seemed to occur to Daisy.

"What strike?" Daisy repeated.

"Jodi's talking about the fact that the maid-chauffeur-cook-cleaning lady at our house resigned due to disrespectful treatment," said Molly as she eyed the donut dish. Another one would certainly taste wonderful. She'd worked up an appetite with all that dancing. But she'd better not, especially with the others watching.

Daisy whooped with laughter. "You've resigned? You're kidding!"

"The kids had gotten so disrespectful to me that I had to do something besides grit my teeth until they left home. But it's not permanent. Only two weeks."

"Ah, that's why he wants to live with us for that long," said Jodi.

"But, Molly, you quit being a mother?" Ardith Jones looked shocked, as Ardith often did. Her matter-of-fact mind had difficulty with imagination and humor and anything unusual. Molly had learned to love her for her unfailing kindness and her faithful friendship in spite of Ardith's black-and-white way of thinking. She understood that this latest adventure must seem very bizarre indeed to Ardith.

"No, I didn't quit being a mom, Ardith. I quit being an unappreciated maid."

"Which means what?" Daisy asked. Her eyes flashed with enthusiasm, and Molly knew Daisy had decided there was hope for Molly after all.

"I'm not doing anything for the kids."

"Nothing?" asked Jodi. "Then Jordan was right. You did quit."

"But your kids are so sweet, Molly," said Ardith. "They really are."

"I agree," said Molly. "They're wonderful to everyone but me."

"All kids are like that," said Jodi.

"That doesn't make it right," Molly said. "God gave me these kids, and I don't want to fail him or them."

"But can you quit like this and not go against Scripture?" asked Ardith, her brow puckered with concern.

"I think so," said Molly. "There really aren't too many express commands to mothers in the Bible. There are plenty of examples of mothers, good and bad, and urgings to children to not forget their mothers' teachings and to honor their mothers. But as far as, 'Mothers, do this, mothers, do that,' it's not there. I looked."

"Perhaps," said Sara, who had been quiet until now, "there are not too many specifics because God wanted to allow for cultural as well as personality differences. After all, the Bible is for all people in all ages in all cultures. By setting down principles but not specifics, God allows for individual circumstances."

"The old principle-pattern thing," said Jodi.

Molly regretfully tore her eyes from the donuts and nodded. "That's what Pete and I thought. The principle I'm fighting for is absolute: 'Honor your father and mother.' My pattern for teaching this principle is mine alone. I mean, there's no way I can go toe-to-toe with the kids to establish my position. I hate confrontation. This way I can make one grand statement instead of the endless, daily, nasty ones."

Ardith still looked unconvinced, but Daisy seemed to understand, as did Sara. Jodi appeared to be reserving judgment.

"It's all Sara's fault," Molly told Ardith with a wicked grin. "She's the one who spelled out the problem to me and encouraged me to do something."

"You encouraged her to go on strike?" Ardith said, aghast that not only had her friend, Molly, lost her mind, but so had her Bible study teacher.

"Well," said Sara with an I'll-get-you look at Molly, "not exactly. I encouraged her to do *something*. This work stoppage is Molly's own idea. And a very interesting one it is. I think that as we begin our study, we'll pray for you and your kids, Molly, okay?"

Molly nodded. It was more than okay. She gladly would take all the prayer she could get. And she thanked the Lord that even if Ardith and Jodi didn't fully understand, they were kinder than her mother had been.

Molly stopped at the Needlework Nook on her way home. She spent an intense half hour studying embroidery threads, carrying clusters of skeins to the front windows to see the colors in natural light. Finally she selected the forest green, celery green, mauve, purple, soft yellow, and cream, along with the black fabric she wanted for her Doxology project.

When she got home, she got out her colored pencils and graph paper and continued plotting the design she had begun the day before.

"I need a computer program for this," she told The Cheshire Cat, asleep in a puddle of sunshine. "It'd make life much simpler."

Molly sat engrossed in her work until Jordan burst in the front door. Suddenly the house vibrated with noise and energy. The cats came awake and quickly began complaining as hunger pangs struck with renewed vigor.

Molly watched Mazeltov and Mike Schmidt circle Jordan as he got some cookies out of the cupboard. The Cheshire Cat stalked Molly, apparently thinking she was a more compliant target.

"What do you think about feeding the cats?" Molly asked.

"Sounds like a good idea," said Jordan, who made no move to do so.

Molly stared at her youngest until he felt the stare and looked at her, frowning.

"What?" he said.

Molly pointed to the cats.

Jordan looked at them, even bending to pet them before it dawned on him what she meant. "You mean I should feed them?"

"Great idea, Jordan."

"All of them?"

"They're all hungry."

"But they're not all mine."

"Do you think you could possibly feed one and not the others?"

He thought for a minute. "They'd fight," he finally decided.

Molly nodded.

"Why me?" Jordan asked.

"Why not you?" Molly countered. "Besides, P.J. and Amie aren't home."

"Um." Jordan looked vaguely at the cabinets.

"The cat food's in the one to the right of the oven," Molly said helpfully.

Stuffing a handful of cookies into his pockets, Jordan went to the cabinet. He pulled out a can and, after several attempts and a threat or two to sue for defective workmanship, finally managed to get the electric can opener to eat its way around the top. He then set the opened can on the floor. Molly could hear his cookies break as he squatted, but he seemed unconcerned about them.

Three cats descended on the food and began hissing and swatting as they jockeyed for position. Jordan watched as he pulled a cookie chunk from his pocket, brushing the clinging lint and a gum wrapper aside before he bit into it.

"You have to divide their food into dishes for them," Molly said. "And quickly, before one of them cuts himself on that lid!"

Sighing, Jordan shoved another handful of cookie fragments into his mouth and retrieved the can, despite the protests of the cats. Wearily he divided the food into three dishes.

"Don't forget that the can's recyclable," Molly said.

"I'm not doing this tomorrow," Jordan said as he pulled the label off the can. "I mean, this is ridiculous!"

"Rinse the can," Molly said. "It needs to be food-free. And put some dried food into another dish, okay?"

When he finished the monumental job of caring for the cats, Jordan stalked off to his room, worn to a frazzle by all his hard work. Humming, Molly began dinner for herself and Pete. She foresaw a quiet if sloppy night at home.

She just hadn't counted on Sherm.

When the doorbell rang about seven-thirty, she went innocently to the slaughter.

"Pop," she exclaimed as she opened the door. She glanced behind him. "Where's Mom?"

"I didn't bring her. I don't want her to be upset by what I'm going to say." His voice was clipped, angry.

Molly's heart began to pound. Another parental confrontation! "Don't tell me you're mad at me, too," she said, shoulders slumped.

"Mad at you? Why would I be mad at you?" Sherm asked as he brought a burst of fresh air inside with him.

"The strike."

"What strike?" He looked confused, then horrified. "Don't tell me there's a strike at the shop!"

"No, of course not. I mean my strike. I thought that's why you came."

He shook his head and almost smiled. "I think your strike is

102

the best joke I've heard in years."

"It's not a joke," Molly said stiffly.

"Maybe not to you," Sherm said. "But I think it's a riot. So does Mom."

"Pop!" said Molly, uncertain whether she preferred being upbraided by her mother or being laughed at by her in-laws.

Sherm stalked into the living room and threw his jacket across the back of the striped chair. Molly did not tell him to hang it up.

"Where is he?" he asked, anger vibrating from him.

And Molly realized why Sherm was here.

"Pop, Pete's taking good care of Gregory Electrical for you. You know he is."

Sherm ignored her. "Where is he?"

Molly sighed. "In the cellar playing Ping-Pong with P.J."

"In the cellar getting creamed by P.J., you mean."

Jordan cruised into the living room and smiled broadly at Sherm. "Hi, Pop-pop."

"Go get your father for me," Sherm ordered.

"Did you hear about what Mom's doing to us?" Jordan dropped into the chair across from Sherm, prepared for a nice, long conversation. Mazeltov leapt into his lap and settled to purring. "Have you come to make her be nice? I bet she'll listen to you."

"I asked you to get your father, young man," said Sherm sternly, his voice hard. "And I meant it."

Jordan looked sideways at Molly, confusion on his face. His grandfather had never spoken to him in such a harsh manner before. He usually reveled in Jordan's bombast and even encouraged him to be outspoken.

"Jordan, do as I say and go get your father!" Sherm threw the boy a look that would have shriveled a hardened criminal, let alone a seventh grader who loved him.

"Jordan, go get your father, please," Molly quietly asked the stunned Jordan. "And why don't you and P.J. stay downstairs and play a few games?"

"I can't stand Ping-Pong," Jordan said automatically.

"Stay down there, boy," snarled Sherm. "You heard your mother. No wonder she went on strike."

Looking as if he'd been slapped, Jordan got up, dumping Mazeltov to the floor. As the cat complained at the rude treatment, Jordan turned blindly to the stairs.

"More than a little feisty tonight, aren't we, Pop?" Molly said as Jordan disappeared from view. "He didn't deserve that tone of voice. It's not him you're mad at."

When she heard what she'd said, she froze, appalled. Never before had she said anything that could be remotely classified as critical of her father-in-law. She and Sherm stared at each other, equally shocked.

"I—I—" stammered Molly. Then she shut her lips firmly. She had been about to apologize, but she suddenly realized she didn't want to. Sherm had been out of line, and she wasn't going to let him off the hook.

Oh, dear, she thought. *Is it my evil twin again?*

Chapter ELEVEN

olly heard Pete slowly ascending from the basement. She could also hear quick, light boy steps racing upstairs. Jordan! She felt a flash of anger at him. Why did he always feel the need to skate on the edge? She hoped he at least had enough sense to stay out of sight if he was choosing to disobey Sherm in his present mood.

She glanced through the living room doorway and saw P.J., not Jordan, sprinting for his room. Suddenly, instead of being angry at her younger son, she felt sorry for him. Poor Jordan, all by himself in the basement.

But, she reminded herself, Pete was the issue now, not Jordan and his hurt feelings.

"Pop," she said, determined to defend her man once again. "Let him do things his way. Give him time. You know he's good at what he does. After all, he learned the business from one of the best."

Sherm raised a skeptical eyebrow and snorted as Pete came into the room.

"I tried to speak with Bud Carson at Arleigh Fabricators this afternoon," Sherm attacked, pulling himself awkwardly out of the enveloping sofa, his arthritic knees giving him a hard time. The struggle to rise to his feet made Sherm all the angrier. He stared belligerently at Pete.

Pete nodded but said nothing.

"He wouldn't talk to me!" Sherm was incredulous. No one had ever before said they wouldn't talk to him. In fact, people wanted to talk to him. People wanted to be in his orbit, to have his prestige and power and charisma rub off on them. People loved him!

When Molly had first met Sherm and Marvella Gregory, she'd been overwhelmed by the man. He was a loud, boisterous person who never met a challenge he didn't like. His energy and enthusiasm for life scared her, though the quiet Marvella and Pete seemed to take him in stride. Of course, they'd had years to get used to him.

On her first visit to the Gregorys' house for a picnic the summer after she and Pete began dating, she had been so anxious that the Gregorys like her that she could barely talk. Her answers to their questions had been monosyllabic, and she had developed a nervous little tic that made her left cheek jump just below her eye.

Part way through the day she had sought the powder room just for its quiet and solitude. She had sat despairing, certain she was disappointing Pete, maybe even losing him by her poor showing. And, worst of all, she had not one idea about how to change herself. Then she had heard voices on the other side of the door.

"She's sort of cute," Sherm said, "in a flat-chested, waifish, quiet sort of way. Different from the blond bombshells you usually bring home."

"She's beautiful, Pop," answered Pete.

Molly glanced in the mirror over the sink and thought Sherm was closer to the truth than Pete.

"Ah," said Sherm, as if he'd had a revelation.

"And she's kind and sweet and funny and gentle and—" Pete paused. "And I think I love her," he finished in an amazed voice.

Molly grabbed the sink and held on to keep from falling. He'd never told her that. She glanced in the mirror again and was startled by the smiling, pretty woman, alight from within, who gazed joyously back.

"Well, son," said Sherm. Molly could hear his slap on the back through the closed door. "Congratulations! But don't ever let me hear that you've been anything but faithful to her or I'll beat you to a pulp. I didn't raise my son to be a skirt chaser. I've loved your mother for twenty-eight years, and I'll admit that sometimes it's been hard. But I believe in commitment. I believe once you say, 'I do,' you can't change your mind." There was a pause, and Molly could almost feel Sherm's hard gaze bearing down on Pete. "And, by George, you'd better believe in it, too."

From that moment on, Molly had loved Sherm. He could still scare her sometimes, but she loved him and Mom. So did everyone else.

She remembered the Chamber of Commerce dinner last year when Sherm had gotten a lifetime achievement award for his service to their town of Remington.

"Good man, your father-in-law," people told her all night. "Really knows what he's doing. Wonderful businessman. Asset to the community."

And at his retirement party a couple months later, the applause had been loud and heartfelt.

"There's never been anybody like Sherm Gregory," the master of ceremonies had said to loud cheers. "And I think we can be thankful for that fact!" Raucous catcalls and warm laughter filled the air.

And now Bud Carson wouldn't talk to him.

Molly remembered an article she had read in which an ex-President of the United States—she couldn't remember which one—had said how strange it was suddenly to go from the seat of power to being an outsider.

"Why, I hadn't even dialed my own phone in years," the man had said. "I barely remembered how."

Pop hadn't dialed his own phone in years either.

"Dad," Pete said. "What do you expect me to do?"

"Dial his phone," said Molly.

"What?" Both men stared at her blankly.

"Sorry," she said in consternation. "I didn't mean to speak out loud." That evil twin again.

Sherm turned from her and attacked Pete once more. "Do you know why he wouldn't speak to me? Do you? His *secretary*—" the scorn in the word told what he thought of having a message conveyed through a mere secretary— "told me you said not to talk to me."

Pete flinched. "Pop, that's not quite the way it went."

"So, how did it go, Peter Michael Gregory, Mr. Big Cheese? Huh? How did it go?"

Peter Michael Gregory, the man with three first names. When Molly first met Pete—when she was a college junior and he a senior—that was the thing she teased him about. Pop's tone tonight was anything but teasing.

"I told him that I was in charge at Gregory Electrical and that the contract he and I had negotiated was a valid and sure thing. There would be no changes or alterations."

"In other words, ignore me!"

Pete said nothing.

"You—" Sherm became red in the face and began breathing so fast he was almost hyperventilating. Molly feared for his blood pressure.

"Pop," Pete said softly. "Did you or did you not announce

your retirement and make a big deal out of giving me the key to the company? Did you or did you not do it in front of two hundred plus witnesses? Or did I just make up, 'It's all yours, Petey boy'? And did you or did you not take me to the lawyers' office where we signed all sorts of transfer-of-ownership papers?"

Sherm's eyes narrowed and he took a deep breath, ready to let fly, when suddenly into the room leaped P.J., arms wide, chest out.

"Ta-da, Pop-pop," he shouted, pride evident in every line of his body. "How do you like it?"

The sight of P.J. in a sorry-looking, washed-out red wrestling singlet with "Remington Raiders" written in weak blue-gray across the chest brought the acrimonious conversation to a roaring halt. Maybe it was the frayed seam under the right arm or the small hole—a cigarette burn?—almost over his heart or the limp shoelace that tied the straps together over his shoulder blades that reduced the room to silence. Whatever it was, the three adults could do nothing but stare.

"What's that awful-looking thing?" Sherm finally asked, his venom redirected.

"Awful-looking?" said P.J., looking down at himself. "It's my varsity wrestling singlet, Pop-pop. They gave them out today."

"They expect you to wear that in front of people?"

"Pop-pop, it's what wrestlers always wear." P.J. looked pained.

"I know what wrestlers wear," Sherm said impatiently. "What I meant was: is your school actually sending you out in public in a uniform so old and awful-looking? Have they no school pride? Or did they give you the worst-looking singlet as a joke because you're the new guy on the team or something?"

P.J. shook his head. "They all look this bad."

"Why?" Sherm demanded.

P.J. shrugged. "I don't know. I guess because no one's bought new ones for years."

"Why not?"

P.J. shrugged again. "Pop-pop, I don't know. Wrestling's not exactly the prime sport in this town, you know."

"Well, I don't pay my taxes for my grandson to go around in an outfit like that. If you're not ashamed to be seen in it, I'm ashamed for you. It's mortifying. The football team and basketball team don't look like that. They're always getting spiffy new uniforms. Their junior varsity teams get new uniforms. For heaven's sake, the marching band looks better than you. Their hats look better than you!"

Jordan peered cautiously into the room, attracted by Sherm's loud voice, which could be heard in three counties.

"They gave you pink uniforms?" Jordan asked, staring at his brother. "With gray letters? I can't believe it. Why would they do that? Pink's a girl's color. The school colors are red and royal. Why a pink singlet with gray letters?"

"It's not pink," P.J. said. "It's red. And the letters are blue."

Jordan made a raspberry. "Very unblue," he said. "Very dead red. Anyone who says differently is color-blind. And have you taken up smoking or something?" He stuck his finger in the hole over P.J.'s heart.

"Get away from me, you twit," P.J. said, slapping at Jordan's hand. "You'll make it worse!"

"I couldn't make it worse," Jordan pronounced.

"I agree," snorted Sherm.

"You look wonderful, P.J.," Molly said, trying to make her voice as warm and encouraging as she could.

"Stupid," said Jordan.

"Wonderful," repeated Molly.

"Idiotic," muttered Sherm.

Molly felt the evil twin rising up inside, ready to speak in defense of her baby.

"Not the kid," said Sherm quickly, seeing the look on Molly's face. "He looks great. In fact, he's grown muscles when I wasn't looking. Lots of them." He smiled proudly at P.J., who smiled happily back. "It's the uniform that's idiotic. Or the condition of it."

"So buy 'em new ones, Pop-pop," said Jordan the Brash. "You're rich."

"Not anymore," said Sherm, glaring at Pete. "I don't have anything anymore. I'm no good anymore. I'm not allowed to be involved anymore. The fact is that I am a has-been, made so by my own son!"

And having thrown a solid barb and thrust it deep into Pete's heart, Sherm grabbed his coat and left without another word.

Out of habit, Molly followed him to the door.

"Good-bye, Pop," she called after him. He didn't respond. She rested her forehead against the storm door and watched until his taillights disappeared.

Slowly she went back to the living room. Pete was standing where she'd left him, shoulders slumped, staring at the floor. The boys had disappeared.

"Are you okay?" she asked.

Pete looked at her with a sad quirk on his lips. She went to him and put her arms around him.

"I'm so sorry, Pete," she said. "Dear God, what do we do now?"

"Amen," said Pete, and she realized she really had been praying.

Chapter TWELVE

Pete sat in his favorite chair on Saturday afternoon as he watched college football. When Molly came in and sat in the rocking chair, she noticed that the football uniforms on the little screen looked bright and new in spite of the dirt smeared all over them. One of the teams even wore real red and true blue.

A far cry from poor P.J.'s uniform, she thought as she spread her Doxology project on her lap.

She laid the color-coded pattern for the design on the end table beside her and mumbled to herself as she counted stitches. Nodding, she pulled from her needle the rich, golden cream thread that had made the grand, gothic *G* and the smaller *O* and *D* of *GOD,* then selected a warm mauve to work in a pattern surrounding it. She would take up the cream thread again later to outline the mauve.

As she made the first diagonal stitch, she grinned. If anything, the piece was turning out more lovely than she'd imagined, the black material looking much richer than the white graph paper she'd drawn the pattern on.

Amie glided into the room and peered over her mother's shoulder.

"That's beautiful, Mom." She glanced at the pattern. "And you designed it? All by yourself? And you picked the colors and everything? You have a very good eye."

Molly decided to ignore the surprise in her daughter's voice and concentrate on the last comment. "Thank you, dear. That's very kind of you."

"Where are you going to hang it?"

"I don't know if I'm going to hang it," Molly said.

"You're going to give it away? But it's so pretty! Why not give it to me? Then you could come into my room any time you wanted to see it."

Molly thought of that room and shuddered. "If or when I hang it, I'll hang it here in the family room. But it's my prototype, so I'll need to take it with me to shops when I try to market my kits."

Amie nodded. "Right. That makes sense. How are you going to frame it?"

"I think I'll double mat it in mauve and cream with an old-fashioned gold frame."

Amie nodded approval. "You know, you ought to get Grandmom to let you sell it—well, not it, but the kits—at the Christmas Cupboard."

A vision of Janis's workroom flashed through Molly's mind and her heart twisted. "I don't know if there'll be a Christmas Cupboard this year."

"What?" Amie was horrified. "There's got to be! It's one of my favorite Christmas things. It sets the mood for all of December."

"Life's tough for Grandmom right now, honey." Talk about stating the obvious. "I don't know if she can pull it off without Granddad."

"But we always help," Amie pointed out. "She won't be

114

doing it alone. And she needs to do it. I mean, after all, life goes on, and she needs to think about people besides herself."

And with that unintentionally callous remark, she left to begin her several-hour-long ritual of getting ready for the youth group party that evening.

Molly wondered about Amie's "She needs to do it." Was that true? Should they pressure Janis to go ahead? Should they say, ever so kindly and encouragingly, "Mom, it's important you do this. It's time to live again."

Or should they be understanding and stand back, let her grieve, take her time?

Dear Lord, is there a right answer here? And what is it?

But even if they got her to agree to go on with the Cupboard, how could Janis ever get enough items together to sell? There wasn't enough time to finish even a small portion of what she usually had, even if she worked from now until show-time without stopping.

But what if Molly finished her Doxology project and maybe a couple others? They'd take up some of the space. Maybe she could even fill one whole room with needlework. Yes, she could do that easily!

She looked around the family room. Several needlework projects hung here, and there were pieces in other rooms as well. She could strip the walls of these originals and use them as examples of her work. She could collect all the pillows and assorted handiwork that she had done through the years and exhibit them. And she could drape her display table with the wedding-ring quilt she'd made that now lay on Pete's and her bed. She could crank out several of the silver-and-gold angels she'd created last year as tree ornaments. And she could take orders for the kits she didn't have time to prepare in advance.

"Mom," she could say, "I'm counting on the Cupboard to launch Molly Gregory Designs."

And Janis would say…

What? What would her mom say?

Talk about an unknown.

"Mother!" Amie's horrified voice ricocheted down the hall, jolting Molly back to the moment and her needle into her thumb.

Molly and Pete shot out of their chairs and raced to the surely injured Amie, Molly sucking her thumb as she ran.

"What?" she asked, her heart pounding. "What?"

"The bathroom!" Amie stood outside the kids' bathroom, pointing a quivering finger. "It's a slime pit! It smells. It reeks. I can't stand it a minute longer!"

Molly sagged against the wall in relief. No one's survival was in jeopardy. It was just life as usual.

Pete glanced at her, his mouth suspiciously twitchy, his eyes dancing.

"Don't you dare laugh," Molly hissed as he turned to go back to the last quarter of his game. Then she turned to look in the offending room, and her own lips began to twitch with a combination of laughter and sympathy.

The room was a mess, all right. The sink was grimy, all gray and blotched and flecked with white and sea green toothpaste blobs. The floor was invisible beneath its multiple-hued towel carpet, which rolled softly like a miniature rural landscape. The bathtub had a soap-scum crust of impressive thickness, and the drain was clogged with enough hair to make a wig. The toilet was growing a pink slime as fascinating as the product of any petri dish.

Over the whole lay an interesting fragrance composed of part damp towel, part sour washcloth, part mildew, and part unflushed toilet.

"Well," said Amie, hands on her hips. "What do we do?"

Molly shrugged as she inspected her pricked thumb. "*We*

don't do anything, but you could clean it."

"Me?" Amie was incredulous. "Me? But I only made part of the mess."

"Then clean your third."

Amie stood for several minutes, staring slump-shouldered at the ruin.

"How come it was never like this before?" she asked.

Molly just looked at her.

Amie glanced at her mother, saw her face, and said, "Oh."

"Oh, indeed," Molly said, adding quickly as Amie turned to head down the hall, "And you can't use our bathroom!"

Amie turned back, looking mutinous. "This is so unfair!"

"And it would be fair to ask me to clean up your mess?" Molly tried to make her voice hard.

Amie looked at her mother through slitted eyes. "I liked you better the old way." Then she took a deep breath and entered the bathroom.

"The cleaning supplies are in the vanity under the sink," Molly offered sweetly.

She thought she heard Amie snarl.

A half hour later, Amie called, "Mom, come here! You've got to see this!"

Molly put her needlework down and went to the bathroom. The room fairly blinded her as the clean surfaces reflected the light.

"Wonderful, Amie," she said, not mentioning the pile of towels heaped behind the door or the empty toilet paper holder or the soapy buildup on the dish. The girl was so pleased with herself and the dazzling effect of her work that Molly decided to let her enjoy the feeling of accomplishment.

Amie sighed with pleasure as she pulled the last clean towel out of the linen closet. "At least I won't have to do that job again for a while."

Molly smiled sadly. Poor, ignorant child.

Three hours later, when she went to perform her final ablutions prior to leaving for her party, Amie let out a shriek.

"All right," she shouted, stalking to the boys' room. "Get into that bathroom and clean up your mess!"

Molly and Pete peered into the bathroom and saw that towels once again carpeted the floor, toothpaste and spit once again streaked the sink, and there was a pool of water on the floor deep enough to swim through. The toilet lid was up and yellow polka dots decorated the porcelain.

"I want to know who the slob is who just brushed his teeth," Amie said, arms crossed martially over her chest. She was staring at P.J.

"Me," said Jordan.

"You?" Amie said in surprise, swinging to face her younger brother. "At five o'clock on a Saturday afternoon?"

Molly was as fascinated as Amie. This was the boy who had to work at remembering to brush before he left for school each morning because he had better things on his mind. Surely he hadn't thought to brush twice in one day, and on a Saturday at that!

"I just realized I hadn't brushed since Thursday morning," he explained to Amie. "My braces were getting crusty."

"You're disgusting!" said Amie, shuddering. "Get in there and get your spit out of the sink. How can I wash my hands in that mess without contracting a communicable disease? And you, P.J., get in there and dry the floor where you didn't shut the shower curtain. Now!"

Jordan and P.J. stared.

"You sound just like Mom," said P.J. without moving from his reclining position on his bed. "And how do you know I'm the one that got water all over the floor?"

"He certainly hasn't washed lately." She indicated Jordan,

who had spent the day digging a hole that was to be the base-ment of a cabin he was building in the woods behind the house, and who was wearing a remarkable amount of the displaced dirt. "Besides, your hair's wet. What are you doing, taking a date to the youth group party?" And she laughed merrily at the absurdity of the idea.

The boys smiled back but still made no move to do as she asked.

She stalked into the room, grabbed Jordan by his shoulder and dragged him from his bed. "Get moving!" She turned on P.J. and reached for him. "You too!" He avoided her by jumping to his feet.

Amazingly, both boys went to the bathroom, albeit reluctantly. They each grabbed a towel from the collection on the floor. P.J. mopped the puddle with his, and Jordan gave the sink a quick swish with his.

Amie nodded approval when they looked at her, then said regally, "Thank you."

"By the way," said P.J., "we're out of clean towels. I had to borrow one of Dad's for my shower."

"Oh no," said Pete with a horrified glance at the moldering pile on the floor. "You may not use any more of ours."

"So what do we do?" P.J. asked.

"You might wash them," suggested Molly.

"Me?" said P.J.

"Why not?" she asked. "You've used your fair share."

He shook his head. "Not me."

"Don't look at me," said Jordan. "I've never worked a washing machine."

"Then you need to learn," said P.J. emphatically.

"And you could teach me?"

Amie waved her hand, dismissing the towels. "I already did more than my part by cleaning this room up," she said.

"Besides, I haven't got any time. I've got to leave right now!"

"I've got to go, too," said P.J.

"You want to ride over with me?"

P.J. shook his head. "I'm not going to church. The guys are picking me up."

"Who?" asked Amie suspiciously. "Not that Zack Callender, I hope."

"What's wrong with Zack? He's a great guy," P.J. said.

"Hah!" Amie's single syllable spoke volumes.

"You just don't know him." P.J.'s jaw had a mutinous set.

"Of course I do," Amie said. "He's been in my class since seventh grade. He's got a terrible reputation!"

"He's been driving me back and forth to wrestling since Mom went off duty," P.J. said. "I've gotten to know him, and I like him."

A horn sounded outside, and P.J. was out the front door before anyone could say anything more.

Pete looked at Amie. "Is he really a bad character?"

"You'd never catch me going out with him," Amie declared.

"Would I ever catch him going out with you?" Jordan asked impudently.

"Just for that, Brace Face, the towels are yours." And Amie stalked to the garage and the car.

Jordan looked thoughtfully at the towels. He shrugged. "I don't need to use one for a couple of days yet. I'm not doing them." And he went to the family room to watch TV.

"Don't even think about it," Pete said as he grabbed Molly's hand and pulled her away from the door. "Besides, it's time to leave for your mother's."

To Molly's relief, Janis was much more welcoming tonight than she had been earlier in the week. She was especially glad to see Jordan, and he was very patient with her hugs and kisses, even slipping an arm around her shoulders for a second and giving her a peck on the cheek before Trojan claimed his attention.

One thing you could say for Trojan, Molly thought as he jumped all over them in his delight at their presence. *He might be overly enthusiastic, but he's consistent, unlike some people I could mention.*

Pete and Janis settled at the kitchen table with all of Janis's financial information. Expecting them to take hours, Molly and Jordan popped in a video to pass the time and sat on the sofa with Trojan between them.

"I don't want you to think you're getting away with something," Molly said to Jordan as the action began. "This movie is an exception because we're at Grandmom's, and I'm making it just for tonight."

Jordan nodded, eyes glued to the opening scenes.

About the time the tenth body keeled over from a lethal blast of torso air conditioning, Molly lost interest. She began planning her contributions to the Cupboard.

There were two works hanging right here in Janis's living room that would be good display pieces in what she now thought of as The Needlework Room. One was a family tree that had been Janis and Ben's Christmas present four years ago. It had taken months to research the genealogical information and months to design and create the colorful, flowing piece.

The other cross-stitch was an old-fashioned sampler, as controlled and linear as the family tree was graceful, as monochromatic in its browns and tans as the family tree was exuberant with color. It contained the alphabet, numbers one through ten, Bible verses, and small running patterns, all making little rectangles within two large vertical rectangles, all very traditional and proper.

Noting that Jordan was glued to his action movie and Janis and Pete were totally involved in their project, Molly went silently up to Janis's workroom, Trojan at her heels. The door was still closed, the lights still off, and the projects still undone.

Molly wandered around the room, looking more closely than she had the other night. As she studied the incomplete projects, a wisp of an idea floated by. She reached for it with delicate fingers, lest it disappear under the pressure of too much thought, and tucked it gently into the base of her brain to retrieve when she had the leisure to turn it this way and that, working the gossamer glimmer of an impression into a solid plan.

She returned to the living room just as Jordan's movie ended. She commandeered the remote and flipped to American Movie Classics, where, in spite of much wailing and gnashing of teeth from Jordan, they watched Fred and Ginger make the remarkable complexity and athleticism of their dances look like kids' play.

"You're smiling at the TV again," Pete said an hour later when he and Janis came into the room.

Molly looked up and nodded.

"I've made a discovery, Dad," Jordan said. "The stupider the movie or show, the more she smiles."

"Spoken like a true twelve-year-old," Molly said.

"You're right," Pete told Jordan. "You should see her during Lawrence Welk reruns."

Jordan gasped, grabbing his throat. "You let her watch that show? Dad, don't you care for her at all?"

"I like Lawrence Welk, too," said Janis. "In small doses."

"Well, yeah," Jordan said. "But you're old."

Molly looked at her mother with great interest. How would she respond to this wonderful piece of tact from her favorite grandson?

Janis smiled wanly. "You're so kind."

Jordan grinned. "Are you broke, Grandmom? Will you be

taking over our room? Do P.J. and I have to sleep in the basement next to the furnace?"

"Not quite." Janis looked relieved, if not exactly happy, at her financial situation. "Pete explained a lot of things to me, and I'm not about to starve. It's just the taxes! They're taking all my money!"

"No more than ever, Mom," Pete said. "You just didn't know about it before."

"I know Dad thought he was being nice to me by not bothering me with money issues, but…" She shook her head sadly. Then she took a deep breath and squared her shoulders. "But enough of this. Come to the kitchen with me, Jordan, and help me cut the devil's food cake I made this afternoon."

Jordan followed her happily, and Molly heard him ask, "Have you started making the sand tarts for the Christmas Cupboard yet? And can I have a couple if you have? To go with the cake, you know."

Janis's answer was inaudible, but Molly thought she knew what it was. Her suspicions were confirmed when they sat at the kitchen table eating Janis's cake and she noticed that Jordan had no sand tarts. Still, she said, "Mom, I think you can help me a lot if you want to."

"Of course I want to, dear, if I can."

Molly swallowed, trying to get her pounding heart back in her chest instead of in her throat. She took off running. "I want to have a room at the Christmas Cupboard for my needlework. I know that you always have more than enough to fill the whole downstairs, but I'm trying to launch a needlework design business. If I had room to display my work and sell kits for some of my pieces, I could start developing a client list. I know that some shop owners come to see what you're offering, and I could follow up with a visit to see about selling Molly Gregory Design kits in their stores. I think I've got things that other people will want to make."

Molly looked at her mother's impassive face and fought back panic. *She's not buying it, not at all. All I need is "Oh?" and I'll cry. I know I will.*

"I just need a place or a venue to let people know the stuff exists," she continued rapidly. If she kept talking, Janis couldn't say no. "I thought you'd be able to offer the ideal situation, especially since I don't have lots and lots yet. One room—we could call it The Needlework Room—wouldn't be too much for me to fill. At least I don't think so. Can you help me? I know it's asking a lot to ask you to give up some of your own space, but I really want to try this. And the Cupboard is the perfect opportunity, don't you agree? Just what I need—"

"Molly!" Janis said.

Molly shut up. She looked around the table and saw Jordan looking at her with an "Okay, enough, Mom" expression on his face. Pete just sat there shaking his head, a wry grin on his face.

"Overkill, huh?" Molly asked.

"Slightly," Janis answered. "But it's okay. I know how you've always loved your needlework. And I also know how beautiful it is. Of course you can have a room—if I do the Cupboard, which I don't think I will."

"Grandmom!" Jordan was clearly shocked. Whether it was over the fact that another of life's constants was changing, or that he probably wouldn't get as many sand tarts as he wanted, Molly wasn't certain.

"Please, Mom," said Molly. "Have it for me? To help me?"

Janis ran her hands through her hair, the picture of uncertainty. "I don't know, honey."

"Grandmom," said Jordan. "I bet the problem is that you don't have Granddad to help you. Well, I've been thinking."

Whenever Jordan said this last line, he'd just had a brainstorm. Molly held her breath as she waited to hear what he would say.

"I know Granddad always collected the money and all for you. Maybe I could do that job? I'm very good in math, and I've got a great calculator, so I can double-check everything. And I can tease the ladies just like Granddad used to. I know I wouldn't be as good or as funny as he was, but I'd still be good enough, I think."

This time it was Janis who cried.

Chapter THIRTEEN

Sunday was an interesting day on several fronts. First there was the matter of the towels.

"Hey," yelled P.J. as he stood dripping after his shower. "What am I supposed to do in here?"

Molly's face showed her empathy as she imagined herself dripping wet and cold, and she automatically reached for one of the towels she and Pete kept in the cabinet under the sink in their bathroom.

"Don't worry," said Pete, taking it from her and putting it back on the shelf. "He's drip-dry. He'll be fine."

And he was. When he showed up at breakfast, he was dry and clothed. Molly could only assume he had used one of the towels carpeting the bathroom floor.

"Used your hair dryer an extra long time, didn't you?" asked Jordan with a grin.

"Shut up," P.J. snarled. "At least it worked without making me smell like a gym. Mom, we've got to get some new towels. Ours stink."

"If you want to use your food money to buy us new towels,

I certainly won't complain," Molly said. "But there's really nothing wrong with the towels we have. They just need to be washed."

Amie glided to the table, still glowing because last night Pastor Paul had told her she looked nice. All those hours of preparation had paid off.

"Did you take a shower this morning?" asked P.J.

"Of course," Amie answered. "What do you think I am, a scuzz like him?" She looked at Jordan.

"Hey," Jordan protested. "Do I look dirty? Do I?"

P.J. grinned at him. "Obviously you can't see the back of your neck."

Jordan squinted his eyes in doubt, and Molly saw him rub the back of his neck when he thought no one was watching. She was glad she wasn't close enough to see the dirt rise about his head like it did around Pig Pen.

"So if you showered, how'd you get yourself dry?" P.J. asked Amie.

"I hung the towel that I used last evening on the closet door in my bedroom so it would dry." She looked surprised, as if she'd discovered one of life's great treasures. "It worked like a charm, and it most certainly didn't stink like some other towels I know."

"Wow!" said Pete. "What a novel idea. Now into the car, all of you, or we'll be late for church."

Word of Molly's work stoppage had spread through the congregation like the proverbial wildfire, and everyone seemed to have an opinion.

"What does Pete think about all of this?" asked Pastor MacMillan when he saw Molly in the hall. He prided himself on keeping a careful eye on his flock for any signs of heresy or need.

"He'd been encouraging me to do something about the kids for quite a while, so he supports me completely," Molly said.

The pastor nodded. "I have to admit that when I first heard about this, I didn't know what to think. But the more I've thought about it, the more it seems to me that, though unorthodox, what you're doing is probably better than the constant yelling and stress that pass for family life in lots of homes. If Pete supports you, I can't find any fault in your actions." Pastor MacMillan was a big supporter of the husband as servant/leader.

Molly was thankful he wasn't perturbed at her, because he had an eyebrow that rivaled Janis's when he was provoked. "I liken my actions to God's withholding things from Israel to remind them to honor him," she explained, trotting out the Scriptural basis for her behavior. "You know—rain, peace. When they repented and changed, then he supplied all their needs again."

Pastor MacMillan looked a bit surprised and, Molly thought, impressed by her comment. "I hope it works out well," he said. "Keep me posted."

"Molly, my dear," said Mrs. Cranston, who had been born with a phone attached to her ear. She cornered Molly in the ladies room between Sunday school and church. "What's this I hear about you deserting your children? I must say, I'm surprised you have the courage to be here this morning after such an ungodly action. I pray God works a miracle in your heart today. As I said to Alma just the other day, I can't believe Molly's been taken in by all the feminist propaganda; though as Vera said, it could happen to anyone. Still, it was a surprise, because, as Betty said and I have to agree, you seemed like such a stable Christian and ideal mother. It's like I reminded Hannah, it's a good thing Pete isn't an elder." And with that non sequitur, she walked away before Molly had a chance to respond.

"Molly, you're my hero," said Pam Swenson, sidling up to Molly in the aisle before church. Pam shook her prematurely gray head at the wonder of it all. Her worried eyes watched her teenaged triplets slump in the pew until they were more lying than sitting. "I just wish I had the nerve. I really do." She turned from Molly to plead, "Come on, kids. Sit up, okay? After all, this is church." The last was a hiss as she climbed, shoulders bent in defeat, over their prone bodies to her seat.

"Are you crazy, Molly?" Audrey Hopp, intense, intelligent, and a great fan of the movie-of-the-week view of the world, waylaid her after the service. "Aren't you afraid your kids will really rebel? Aren't you afraid they'll run away? Aren't you afraid they'll get involved in drugs?" She leaned in and whispered, "Or sex?"

Molly, who had never considered that her strike might lead to such eventualities, smiled weakly.

Nodding her head with grim satisfaction, Audrey continued, "And aren't you afraid they'll resent you for trying to control them, maybe resent you for the rest of their lives? All that hidden anger boiling up at stressful times." She shook her head. "You see it all the time, you know. Just last week there was this movie on television—the daughter ran away because the mother was too strict. She became a prostitute!"

Molly blinked. "Who—the mother or the daughter?"

Audrey was looking at her strangely when they were joined by Jane Scaringi, a forty-year-old spinster who considered herself the church's expert on child rearing.

"If you'd stayed on top of the situation, Molly," Jane said crisply, "none of this would have been necessary. Be honest with yourself, Molly. There must have been a laxness, an ignoring of your responsibilities, an unwillingness to fulfill your motherly duties somewhere through the years. All you need to do is look them in the eye and say, 'You heard me. Now do it.'"

"You learned this from all your experience with children?" Molly asked, the evil twin surfacing.

Jane snorted. "I read, Molly. I read."

"Ah," Molly said, adding with exaggerated goodwill and the sweetest smile she could muster, "well, I thank you, both of you, Jane and Audrey, for your gracious encouragement and prayerful support. I can't imagine where I'd be without caring friends like you two."

The women blinked in surprise.

Oh, Lord, forgive me, Molly prayed as she walked up the aisle. *But enough is enough!*

It was an unexpected pleasure to see the kids all together in the vestibule, and she hurried to herd them out before anyone else stopped her to share an opinion. But she wasn't quite fast enough.

"Of all the foolish things I've ever heard of," a loud, accusatory male voice said from behind her. She turned to find Tim Wenger, the congregation's self-appointed confronter and arch conservative staring at her from behind his dashing and out-of-character mustache. His mousy, browbeaten wife, Emily, lurked at his side. "The Bible says, Molly, that a mother's place is at home with her kids."

Molly, P.J., Amie, and Jordan looked at each other, then at Mr. Wenger in confusion.

"I am at home with my kids, Tim," Molly said with more acid than she'd intended. She was rapidly nearing the end of her very long rope. And where was Pete when she needed him?

"At home *caring* for them, Molly," Tim said so loudly that heads turned. "You should be ashamed. Reneging on your God-given responsibilities! Where's that quiet and gentle spirit Paul says you should have? A bad mother is a bad testimony."

P.J. slid his arm around Molly's shoulders, and Amie and Jordan moved protectively close.

"She's not a bad mother at all, Mr. Wenger," said Amie.

"Just the opposite," said P.J.

"And she's a great cook," said Jordan, who then ruined it by adding, "when she cooks."

Molly glowed.

Later in the day the towels struck again. Molly, Pete, and the boys were in the family room watching football when, during an advertising break, P.J. left the room. Moments later, Molly heard the washing machine start.

Her heart swelled with pride. Her strike was working! The boy was shouldering a previously unassumed responsibility and no one had nagged anyone.

"P.J.," she said when he returned to the room, "are you by any chance washing the towels?"

He nodded. "I figured I'd need one tomorrow morning. I don't have the time to dry myself with my hair dryer every day, you know. You'd be surprised at how uncomfortable and time-consuming that is. Dangerous, really. You could burn yourself in very sensitive areas. So I decided I'd just wash it." And he grinned.

"Good going, P.J.," said Jordan.

Molly sat back, almost euphoric. It was five plays later before she processed completely what P.J. had said, and her pride bubble burst big time.

"You decided to wash it? It?" she demanded. She jumped up and hurried to the laundry room. When she threw the lid of the washing machine up, her worst fears were confirmed. There, in a machine full to the brim with gallons of super-sudsy water, was a lone towel, waving like a strand of kelp in a gentle, foaming sea.

She stalked into the living room, trying to figure out where she had gone wrong to have raised such a selfish, thoughtless son. And he was the considerate one of the bunch!

"One towel?" she said through gritted teeth. "You're washing one towel?"

"One towel?" echoed Jordan. He looked as hurt as he had

the first time P.J. went to a junior high social outing at church and he couldn't go along.

"What do you mean, I can't go for three more years?" he had wailed in the car after they dropped P.J. off. "That means he's going to get to go to things three more years than I am. It's not fair." And his eyes filled with tears at the perfidy of it all.

Now he looked at his idolized big brother and said with great sorrow, "You mean you're not washing any towels for me and Amie? Only you?"

P.J. looked genuinely startled. "Why should I do yours? I figured you'd take care of your own."

"One towel at a time?" Molly heard the nasty screech in her voice. She put out her hands to push away the anger and took a few deep breaths to calm herself. She was much more frustrated than the severity of the crime warranted, and she needed to get control of herself.

When she was calmer, she asked, "What about the waste of water? And detergent? Do you think we can really afford for everyone to wash one towel at a time?"

"Oh."

"You mean 'Oh?'" said Jordan helpfully and was rewarded with both his mother and brother looking daggers at him.

Molly turned back to her older son. "Go get the other towels, P.J. I left the lid up so the machine will wait for you and a full load. Just add the towels slowly or you'll have a mess with water sloshing all over the place. And remember, both of you, that you always either have a full load or adjust the water level for a smaller load."

Several hours later, when P.J. was ready to go to bed, Molly decided to ask, "Did you ever put the towels in the dryer?"

He looked momentarily startled, then grinned. "Wouldn't do us much good to have clean towels if they were still wet, now would it?"

It was the next morning when P.J. discovered he had no clean underwear and rushed back to the laundry room, fresh towel around his waist.

"One pair," he mumbled over and over as he launched an intensive search. "One pair is all I need. Mom!" The last cry was desperate.

Molly came to the laundry room.

"I haven't got any clean underwear!" P.J. said.

Molly nodded.

"And there aren't any out here!"

Molly nodded again. "That's because I always carry the folded items to your rooms, not like some other people I could name," she said, pointing to the towels hanging like green and coral tongues from the dryer door.

"But what am I supposed to do?"

"Start a load—a full load—I guess."

"But that doesn't help me now! And I need help now!"

"I guess you'll have to wear something over again."

"What?" He shuddered fastidiously at the thought, an interesting response, Molly thought, for a kid who spent his after school hours grappling with sweaty guys, their noses frequently in very unsavory spots of each other's anatomy.

P.J. nodded decisively. "I'll just have to borrow a pair from Dad."

"You can ask," agreed Molly. She was amazed and delighted at her aplomb in the face of P.J.'s agitation.

I don't even feel guilty, she thought. *I'm not responsible for his quandary; he is, and he knows it!* She grinned mentally. *I'm getting good at this!*

"Mom," said P.J. earnestly, retucking his towel about his waist as it threatened to yield to the law of gravity. "Don't you think this plan of yours has gone far enough?"

"When you do your wash," said Molly in response, "don't mix

your darks and whites, add only one cap full of detergent—yesterday you added way too much—and adjust the water level button as needed."

"I don't really want to wash clothes," said P.J. through clenched teeth. "I will live happily ever after if I never wash clothes."

Molly shrugged. "Your choice."

"Mom, this isn't fair!"

"P.J., fair isn't what we're after. Godly is. Responsible is."

Sighing mightily, P.J. got his hamper, dragged it to the laundry room, and dumped it into the washer.

"You'd better sort that stuff," she said as she saw jeans and a bright crimson Remington sweatshirt fall out.

"If I'm doing this, I'm doing it my way," he growled

"If you like pastel underwear, be my guest." Molly left him and returned to the kitchen.

His grousing was barely audible over the noise of his none-too-gentle treatment of the washing machine as he pulled his dark clothes out and threw them in a heap on the floor.

"He should do as I do," Jordan suggested to Molly. He was shoveling in Corn Pops at an incredible speed. "If you wash yourself every other day, you only have to change underwear every other day, and it lasts twice as long."

Molly cringed and made believe she hadn't heard him.

Chapter FOURTEEN

Wednesday evening found everyone in the kitchen area. Molly and Pete were seated at the table, eating Chinese takeout. Molly had taken one look at the counters and called Pete to stop at Chan's Chinese Chow on his way home.

Partially consumed food, glasses with residue the consistency of tar, every piece of flatware in the house, pans whose nonstick lives were over, and numberless dishes cluttered every available surface, many layers deep. The melted ice cream container still sat in the sink with various utensils and dishcloths hanging out of it, giving off an odor that warned of unimaginable health horrors.

Oh, Lord, she prayed as she surveyed the mess, *please protect them from botulism or salmonella.*

As Pete tucked into his shrimp with lobster sauce, he reported on his day.

"Bud Carson and I signed the official contract for our work at the new Arleigh plant." He looked slightly delirious at his coup. "He took me out to lunch at that expensive new restaurant over by the country club. I had the greatest steak salad."

"Steak salad?"

"With French fries in it, no less."

"Well, congratulations, honey," Molly said, pleased to see Pete so pleased. "I'm delighted for you. I take it Pop didn't interfere anymore?"

Pete's smile dimmed. "I haven't heard from Pop since he left here in a snit last week."

"He hasn't even come to the office?"

Pete shook his head. "And I feel guilty because I feel so relieved."

Molly took a bite of her egg roll lathered in a mixture of duck sauce and hot mustard. As her eyes began to water and her sinuses cleared, she hastened to add more duck sauce to the mixture. "You need to call him," she said in a gasp, due to the aftereffects of the hot mustard.

Pete nodded glumly. "I know," he said, watching the kids try to prepare their dinners and succeed only in getting in each other's way.

"Come on, Amie," Jordan whined. "Cook mine? Please?"

Amie shook her head decisively.

"You still can't read directions?" asked P.J. "Move over, Amie. You're in my way."

"That's my dish, P.J. I just washed it." Amie retrieved the clean Corelle plate none too gently. "And I've been meaning to ask you—are you still riding back and forth to school with Zack Callender?"

"I am," P.J. said. "And I think you don't like him because he doesn't like you."

"He doesn't like me?" Amie stared at P.J. "I didn't even know he knew I was alive."

"He knows," smirked P.J. "Miss Goody Two Shoes is what he calls you."

"Probably only when he's around you and minding his language," Amie said. "And knowing him as I do, I consider that a great compliment."

"Tell me more about this guy," said Pete as he speared some of Molly's pork lo mein.

"He's a foul mouthed creep who makes my skin crawl," said Amie.

"He's an okay guy, Dad," said P.J. "He talks a bit locker room, but he's cool."

"Ha!" said Amie. "He's a boozer who loves getting himself and others into trouble."

"Why don't you bring him over, P.J.?" said Molly. "I'd like to meet the guy who's taking over my duties as your driver."

"No, you wouldn't," said Amie. "Believe me."

"He's pretty busy," said P.J. "But I'll see if he's got a free night sometime soon."

"Let me know ahead of time so I can be out of the house," said Amie. "It's bad enough I have to see him at school. I don't want to share my home with him."

Pete looked thoughtful. "P.J., you may have to ride to and from practice with him, but I think I'll ask you not to do anything social with him until Mom or I get to meet him. I don't want you hanging around with some underage drinker."

P.J. looked pained. "Dad, he's an okay guy."

"Maybe," Pete said. "Let's just meet him and make our own judgments, okay?"

Jordan was clearly bored with the subject of Zack Callender. "Who's making this salad?" he demanded, looking at a head of crisp lettuce balanced on top of a nearly empty glass of milk of highly suspect wholesomeness. "And who got these cucumbers and tomatoes and cheese? They look so good!"

"It's all mine," said P.J., "and don't you dare touch one little thing. I just got desperate for something besides a TV dinner."

"I know," said Jordan. "School lunches are even starting to

look good." He eyed his brother and continued hesitantly. "Could you make me a salad? And some of that hamburger stuff you're cooking?"

P.J., who seemed to be discovering that cooking could be fun, looked thoughtfully at his little brother. "What'll you give me in exchange?"

"A trade?" Jordan's voice was excited. "How about you make my dinner and I wash your dishes?"

"And your dishes, too?" P.J. asked.

Making a face, Jordan looked with longing at the lettuce and the bubbling hamburger. He capitulated. "Okay. I'll wash my dishes, too."

"Deal," said P.J. "Go stick a couple of pieces of bread in the toaster. We need them to put the stroganoff on."

"Stroganoff? We're going to have stroganoff? Wow!"

"Geez, you're easy to impress, kid," Amie said as Jordan rooted through the counter chaos for a loaf of bread. She turned to P.J. "And where did you ever learn to cook something like stroganoff?" She leaned in to watch as he dumped a can of mushroom soup into the hamburger.

"See that?" P.J. asked, pointing to Betty Crocker balanced precariously on the flour canister. "It's called a cookbook. It tells you how to do things with food. You might find it worth opening some day."

"Very funny," said Amie who showed no interest in even looking at the book, let alone opening it.

P.J. opened a container of sour cream and added it to his masterpiece, humming as he stirred. Jordan retrieved the toast and brought it to his brother.

"What about me?" asked Amie, who apparently had nothing for dinner except her clean plate. "Make me a salad and some stroganoff, too?"

P.J. glanced at her. "What'll you give me?"

140

Amie thought for a minute. "How about a clean counter to work on?"

"You mean you'll wash this stuff? All of it?" He indicated the mind-boggling mess.

"If you'll make my dinner. And if he'll wash my dishes afterwards."

Amie and P.J. looked at Jordan to see how this idea appealed. Obviously it didn't.

Détente hangs in the balance, thought Molly as she and Pete watched.

P.J. held the cheddar he planned to shred for the salad under Jordan's nose. Then he lifted the pan of gently simmering hamburger and waved it in front of his brother. Molly could almost see Jordan begin to salivate.

"Oh, okay," he said with an utter lack of grace. "I'll do your stupid dishes."

P.J. and Amie nodded approval as P.J. turned off the heat under the hamburger.

"Call us when the counters are clean," he said. "Jordan and I will be in the living room."

"What?" Amie was aghast.

"You said you'd clean the counters for me to work on," P.J. said. "So when you clean them, I'll work on them. Until then, I'm watching TV."

Amie stared after her brothers as they walked out on her.

"Mom!" she complained. "Dad! Make them come help me!"

Pete swallowed his fried rice and said, "You said you'd clean the counters, Amie. We all heard you."

"But...but..." she sputtered, looking at the clutter without the vaguest idea how to fix it.

"If you can conquer the bathroom, you can conquer the kitchen," said Molly with an encouraging smile. "Why not start by putting away the food?"

"You're gloating, aren't you?" Amie accused, scowling at her parents. "I can tell. You actually think you've won. Well, I might have made one mistake, but they won't get me again. And neither…" she paused, "will…" then paused again, "you!"

With as many slammed cabinet doors and banged-down cans as she could manage, Amie began putting the food away.

Molly broke open her fortune cookie. *Good times await you,* it read.

I sure hope so, she thought as she watched Amie search for the dish detergent, which was right in front of her—exactly where Molly had left it in case anyone was ever inclined to wash a dish. *I sure hope so.*

"I'm finished," Amie finally sang out, forcing the last dish into the dishwasher. P.J. came from the living room to check out her work, turning the heat under the hamburger back on as he passed the stove.

"Oh no, you're not," he said as he moved to block her from exiting the room.

"I am so," Amie said as she scanned the cleared counters.

"You said clean counters to work on," P.J. said. "The dishes may be in the dishwasher, but the counters are hardly clean."

"Come on," said Amie plaintively. "Give me a break."

P.J. shrugged. "No food then," he said as he turned to stir the hamburger.

Looking angry enough to spout fire, Amie grabbed a handful of paper towels and began vigorously pushing anything remaining on the counter toward the sink and the ice cream container.

"Good idea, Amie," said Molly. "You can dump any refuse in the ice cream container and take it all to the garbage can in the garage in one quick trip."

Amie turned steely eyes on her mother. "I thank you," she said frostily. "What a deep and insightful suggestion."

Molly sighed. *Good times await me, oh yeah.*

The doorbell rang as Molly finished the last stitch she needed to make in celery green. The little ivy leaves that twined around the letters of the Doxology looked almost lifelike with their bicolor scheme of half forest and half celery. She laid her work aside and pulled herself from her rocker while Pete read the paper and the kids lounged about the family room watching TV.

"Don't move. It's okay," Molly said loudly to them all. "I'll get it."

No one heard her any more than they'd heard the bell. Or at least acknowledged they'd heard it. It was amazing that all the family except her suffered from that pernicious disease, *deafness convenientus*.

"Pop," she said uncertainly when she saw Sherm standing beneath the porch light. "And Mom." Relief coursed through her as she saw Marvella. No confrontations tonight. "Come on in."

"I've come to see P.J.," Sherm announced as they slipped off their coats. "Where is he?"

"In the family room."

"Are you still on strike?" he asked.

Molly nodded.

"I told you she'd make it last," said Marvella. "You think quiet people give up on things, but you're wrong."

"First time," said Sherm, grabbing the handful of sales brochures and catalogs he'd brought with him.

"Look what I got for you, kid," he said enthusiastically as he surged into the family room. He dropped the whole collection on P.J.

P.J. grabbed a catalog and began leafing through it. Jordan grabbed another.

"Hello to you, too, Pop," said Pete as he got up and gave his mother a kiss. "It's good to see you."

"Shush," said Marvella. "Let him alone. He's interested!"

"What?" said Pete.

"He's interested."

"These are uniform catalogs," said P.J.

"Wrestling uniforms," said Sherm. "See there?"

P.J. nodded as he looked where Sherm pointed. "But what's the point, Pop-pop?"

"We're going to get you a uniform that's not an embarrassment."

For a moment, P.J. looked delighted. Then he said, "But I can't get a uniform that's different from everybody else's. I mean, we're a team."

"Sure, sure," said Sherm. "I know. We're going to get all of you new uniforms."

"All of us new uniforms?" P.J. repeated.

"And sweats."

"The whole team new uniforms? And sweats?" Pete rubbed his forehead as though he had a headache. "But, Pop—"

"Hush, Pete," said Marvella, poking her son in the arm. "He's interested."

"I told you you should buy them," said Jordan. "I knew you were rich enough."

"Not me, Jordan," said Sherm. He paused for the full dramatic effect. When everyone, even Amie, was looking at him, he continued, "I've been talking to different businessmen in town about the scandalous condition of the Remington wrestlers and their equipment, and I've got a wrestling Boosters Club all organized."

"Pop-pop!" P.J. looked from the catalog to his grandfather. "You're serious! We're going to get decent uniforms! And mats? And head gear?"

"You don't have good mats?" Sherm looked distressed.

"Awful!" P.J. said.

"We'll get good mats, too. And anything else you boys need. I haven't been in every civic organization in Remington all these years for nothing! I know which businesses to approach."

"But, Pop," began Pete again.

"Hush, Pete," repeated Marvella, poking him in the ribs this time and with enough *umph* to make him jump and rub his side. "Let the boy enjoy! *He's interested!*"

"Who's interested?" asked Molly, slightly confused. "In what?"

Pete spoke again. "I was just going to ask, Pop, if you'd spoken with Mr. Davenport about this."

"Who's he?" asked Sherm.

"He's my coach," P.J. said.

"Why should I speak to him? You think he'll tell me not to collect money for his team? And why hasn't he gotten these boys decent stuff, I'd like to know," Sherm said, obviously judging the man and finding him wanting.

"He's tried, Pop-pop," said P.J. "He went to the athletic director just last week about mats, but he was told there wasn't any money."

"Well, there is now." Sherm turned to Pete. "Of course, Mr. CEO, I'm counting on Gregory Electrical to make a hefty donation."

Pete looked pained but said bravely, "We'll certainly do our part, Pop."

Molly welled up with joy—Sherm really had given the business over to Pete. Really given it over.

"You know," Sherm went on. "This whole uniform fiasco has gotten me thinking a lot recently about the condition of the educational system in this town."

"For three whole days," muttered Marvella. "But I'm not

knocking this great new concern of his. I'm too thankful he's interested!"

Sherm continued, "I went to the district administrative offices the other day and got a copy of the budget. I wanted to know how they were spending their money if they couldn't even outfit their teams. And I'll tell you, Pete, I wasn't impressed."

"A school district the size of Remington is a big business, Pop, a multi-million-dollar business. How can you analyze their finances that quickly?"

Sherm ignored the question. "Do you know who's on our school board? Two mothers, a car salesman, a teacher who teaches in another district, a retired minister, and a civil engineer. Now, I ask you, what do any of them know about running a business?" He sighed. "I think I'm going to have to run for school board at the next election just to get a business person serving."

"Pop!" Pete looked floored, though why, Molly wasn't quite certain. Sherm was always taking on one cause or another. One year he revitalized the Lions' Club. Another year he was chief fund-raiser for the local YMCA's building drive. And then there was the year he talked the town council into planting flowering cherry trees all along Main Street because Marvella happened to mention that flowering shrubs made any street look lovely—which Main Street wasn't. The school board was just another place to flex his admirable, if strong-arm, administrative abilities.

"I think it's great that you want to be on the school board, Pop-pop," said Jordan. "Then you can give us longer vacations."

"Not a bad idea," said Sherm. "Do you think I can make that part of my platform?"

"Not if you want the parents to vote for you," mumbled Pete.

"Pop," said Molly, "I think the state mandates the number of days the kids have to attend classes."

"Really?" said Sherm. "Sorry, Jordan. It looks like I'm going to have to let you down on that one."

"Pop," said Pete. "You can't be on the school board. You don't know anything about education."

"Pete," said Marvella, her voice very firm. "Don't interfere with your father's plans. I'm sure he'll be a great asset to the school board. And he's interested!"

"But, Mom!" Pete spread his hands and wrinkled his forehead in disbelief.

Poor Pete, Molly thought. The idea of his dad controlling the educational process in Remington was beyond him.

Marvella looked at Sherm, saw him engrossed in the catalogs, and hissed, "Peter Michael Gregory, shut up! He's interested in something besides organizing me!"

"Is his retirement giving you trouble?" asked Molly sympathetically.

Marvella shuddered. "I've got to get him out of the house or I'll go nuts! He seems to think I have nothing to do but be at his beck and call. He forgets that I have a life of my own that I want to keep living!"

"He's only ever been home on Saturdays and Sundays and holidays," said Molly. "He undoubtedly thinks all your days are like that."

Marvella shook her head. "Well, they're not. I go to the Y to swim; I belong to a bridge club; I'm in some civic organizations; I direct Meals on Wheels. And I want to continue doing it all! I tell you," and she shook her head in pure frustration, "I don't know why the divorce rate doesn't skyrocket at sixty-five. I know he was driving you crazy at work, Pete, but I was so glad he was bothering you instead of me."

"Come on, Mom. It can't be that bad," said Pete placatingly.

"Look me in the eye and say that," Marvella challenged. "Why, last week he reorganized my kitchen cupboards, and I still haven't found where he put my favorite pans. Of course he can't remember. Yesterday he cleaned our bedroom closet and threw away two of my favorite dresses. And—" she drew herself up to pronounce the final outrage— "he expects me to make lunch when *he's* hungry instead of when I'm hungry or when it's convenient."

Molly couldn't help but smile, and Pete gave his mother a bear hug. "Poor Mom."

"So you can see, Pete, I'm sure Remington will survive having him on the school board better than I'll survive having him at home!"

Chapter FIFTEEN

Hi, Mom," Molly said, smiling as she stood in front of Janis's front door on Saturday morning.

"Molly!" Janis smiled back, holding on to Trojan's collar. "Did I know you were coming?"

Molly shook her head. "I decided it would be more fun to surprise you."

She held out her hand toward Trojan, who surged toward her. Janis had to let go or dislocate her shoulder. The freed Trojan gave Molly his most ardent and wet welcome as he draped his forepaws over her shoulders. Planting her sneakered feet far apart, she let him wash her neck and ear.

"Hey, Grandmom," Amie called as she ran up Janis's front walk.

Janis opened her front door wider to greet the girl and for the first time noticed other cars pulling into her driveway. She looked at Molly. "What's going on?"

Molly took a deep breath. She was perspiring from the tension that gripped her, her armpits wet despite her antiperspirant. She looked hesitantly at her mother over Trojan's shoulder. "They're my Bible study friends."

"Your Bible study friends?" Janis was flummoxed.

"Plus me," said Amie. "We've come to help you."

"Help me? Help me how?"

"With your Christmas Cupboard," said Amie.

Molly watched Janis's face closely as Amie talked, and she had no trouble reading the confusion. So far there was no anger, but she had no doubt it would come.

"Please let your mom know we're coming," Sara had said when the women from her Bible study agreed to help her with her plan to salvage Janis's life. "I don't think she'll be too happy with you if we just show up."

But Molly hesitated.

"Do you think I should tell her we're coming?" she'd asked Pete last night as she sat on the bed and watched him pack for the men's retreat.

"No," she answered herself before he had an opportunity to respond. "If I tell her, she'll just tell us not to come."

"If you don't tell her, she'll get mad—and justifiably so," Pete cautioned, stuffing underwear and a sweatshirt into his gym bag. He grabbed some socks and a couple of long-sleeved T-shirts. "You'll be invading her privacy, revealing her difficulties to strangers."

"But when she sees how much we're helping her, she'll get over it. She'll be glad." She looked at Pete for confirmation. "Won't she?"

He shrugged and shoved a pair of shorts and a pair of jeans into the bag. "I can't help you, Molly. Janis is sort of hard to read these days."

Molly nibbled at her nails. "If I tell her, she'll just say, 'Oh?' I can't tell her!"

Pete held his razor and shaving tackle in his hand. He studied them for a minute, then returned them to their shelf. "I'm declaring independence from the tyranny of the blade, at least for the weekend. And I repeat: I think you should call your mom." He dropped his Bible, toothbrush, and toothpaste on top of his clothes, and, with great flourish, zipped his bag shut. Then he pulled his navy anorak over his head.

Molly stared in amazement. "You're all packed? Already?"

Pete nodded. He reached out and pulled her hand away from her mouth. "Moll, stop biting your nails and call her."

"They're my nails," said Molly, purposely ignoring the real point. "If I want to bite them, I should be allowed."

"Then how about waiting until I leave home? Then you can bite them to the quick, if you please. I just won't have to watch you."

"Is it any worse for you to watch me bite my nails than it is for me to listen to you and the boys have belching contests? I think not."

"Belching contests are manly," Pete said. "Biting nails is simply silly. Now give me a kiss good-bye. Show me how much you're going to miss me."

"I promise to miss you," she said as she wrapped her arms around his neck. "I promise to have difficulty sleeping because you're not beside me."

"You always have difficulty sleeping," Pete said. "That doesn't mean a thing."

"Then how about this?" And she kissed him hard.

"Oh, yeech," said a voice. "I come to offer to carry your bag, and what do I see? It's enough to traumatize a sensitive kid like me."

Molly and Pete looked up to see Jordan in the doorway. Molly started to step back, but Pete pulled her closer and kissed her again. When he finally released her, he swatted her gently on the bottom.

"Son," he said to Jordan as he handed over his bag, "I hope that you always enjoy kissing your wife as much as I enjoy kissing mine."

"But Dad, that's my mom you're manhandling."

Pete eyed Molly. "Don't I know it."

Molly smiled at Jordan's pained expression. Like most twelve-year-olds, he liked to think he was immaculately conceived because the alternative was too difficult to imagine.

The whole family walked Pete to the car. The last thing he said to Molly was, "And call your mother."

But she hadn't called. She'd decided to risk possible anger with her friends around to ease the situation rather than face certain anger by telling Janis her plan beforehand. But now the moment of truth was actually here, and as usual she doubted her own decision.

Dear Lord, please help it go okay!

"You're here to help me with the Christmas Cupboard?" Janis asked as she watched Molly's friends walk toward her door. "But it's not Christmas Cupboard time for a couple of weeks yet."

"Oh, we know," said Amie. "We've come to help you get ready."

"What?" Janis looked from Amie to Molly to the women now standing on her doorstep. Molly could see panic beginning to replace the confusion. Janis gripped the doorjamb, her knuckles white.

"It's okay, Mom," Molly said gently.

The fierce look Janis shot Molly turned her mouth dry. Not panic. Anger. Molly swallowed convulsively.

"Grandmom," said Amie, walking into the house, never for a moment considering that they might not be welcome, "I want you to teach me how to make those little angels with the draped skirts. You know the ones I mean? You use glue or something to make their robes stiff."

Janis automatically followed Amie. Sara, Jodi, Daisy, and Ardith followed Janis. Molly came last, holding Trojan, who was desperate to share his affectionate heart with each of the women as they passed him.

When she allowed the dog to pull her into the house, Molly went immediately to the powder room, Trojan traipsing after her happily. This was a place where he got some of his best scratches.

Quickly Molly slipped by him. She backed out of the room and shut him in before he could get his big body turned about in the small space. She leaned against the door to hold it shut as he jumped against it, vociferously proclaiming his opinion of her treachery.

Talking loudly to be heard over Trojan's barking, Molly introduced her friends to her mother. Janis nodded politely, if distantly. As Molly had anticipated, her sense of propriety prevented her from saying what she was thinking.

"I can't tell you how excited I am to be here," gushed Jodi. "I've come to the Christmas Cupboard for the past several years, and I consider it a great honor to help you prepare."

Molly stared at the usually cool Jodi in surprise. So did Janis, and Molly could see that the compliment was having a positive effect.

"Thank you," Janis said with a small smile.

Amie was already upstairs, throwing open Janis's workroom and turning on the lights.

"I'm not very clever with my hands," said Ardith as she walked upstairs beside Janis. "That's why I brought the lunch." She pointed to the cooler she and Jodi had lugged in. "But I can help inventory things or price things or clean up after everybody." She smiled earnestly. "You just tell me what to do and I'll do it."

It said a lot for the size of the room Ben had created for his wife that the seven of them did not crowd the space. Janis stood in the doorway with a stiff, polite smile pasted on her face and waited while strangers saw the evidence of her emotional chaos. The pink patches on her pale cheeks were the most obvious indicators of her embarrassment and anger, and Molly noticed Janis's arms were crossed over her body, her fingers digging into the flesh of her upper arms.

"What a wonderful room," said Daisy. "Wouldn't I love a workspace this large!"

"What do you do, Daisy?" asked Janis politely.

"I'm a free-lance editor, and my company's called Red Pencil Enterprises. I've got all my equipment and supplies squeezed into what amounts to a large closet. I get claustrophobic if I have to stay in it too long." She spread her arms wide. "Something like this would be absolutely wonderful!"

"My husband designed and made it for me." said Janis.

"Well, it's obvious he loved you very much," said Ardith with a sweet smile.

"Okay, Mrs. Eberly," said Sara into the small silence that followed Ardith's remark, "put us to work."

Unclenching her teeth, Janis slowly began giving instructions. Jodi got the clothespins and greens, Sara the grapevine wreaths, and Amie the little angels. Molly was assigned the dried flower arrangements.

She took a basket and began arranging the flowers as artistically as she could. She had an adequate eye for composition and color in such work, but nothing to rival her talent in needlework design, and nothing near the caliber of her mother's ability with flowers. She looked at her finished product and shook her head, dissatisfied. It had all the grace of a bunch of pencils stuck in a holder.

Suddenly she heard Janis laugh. She looked up, startled and

pleased. Janis and Sara were working together on a grapevine wreath, hot gluing silk flowers into an explosion of spring blooms.

Janis seemed to feel Molly's glance. She turned to her daughter and the joy fled her face.

"Here, Molly," she said coolly as she crossed the room. "Let's try it this way."

She added some purple statice and baby's breath to the arrangement. Then she pulled a couple of stems of milkweed pods free and snipped off the ends. When she reinserted them, the new height was exactly right. She took some cockscomb, snipped again and tucked it in the front, just a hair off-center, then wrapped the lip of the basket in a delicate swag of Spanish moss. Suddenly an adequate arrangement had become wonderful.

"Beautiful, Mom."

Janis looked at her coldly, eyebrow cocked. "Thank you. Put those dried hydrangeas in that basket, would you? And use that ribbon." Janis pointed to a spool of crimson-and-gold brocade.

Molly nodded. She could do that. Years ago, Janis had taught her how to make bows. She looped the ribbon and twisted some wire and, abracadabra, she had a rich-looking bow with long streamers. She began placing the faintly pink hydrangeas, taking care not to squash them. She was looking with distaste at the resultant mass, which bore an uncanny and unattractive resemblance to a dish of butter pecan ice cream, when Amie appeared at her shoulder.

"Look, Mom. Isn't this cool?" She held out a miniature angel about four inches high. A robe of pink-and-gold brocade was draped elegantly from its wire shoulders. The material was still wet with glue, and as Molly watched, Amie tweaked it a little here and a little there. Suddenly, the angel looked ready to fly away.

"How did you do that?" Molly asked.

"Do what?" said Amie.

"Make her look like she could fly."

Amie shrugged. "I don't know. I just did what needed to be done."

Molly studied her daughter thoughtfully for a minute. Then she thrust the unfortunate basket of hydrangeas at her. "Can you fix this?"

Amie looked at the basket and nodded. "No problem. They're too pushed together." Quickly she rearranged a couple of the flowers. "They need to feel more fluid, less clumpy."

"Less clumpy?"

"That's right," Amie said. "Less clumpy. Is this the bow?" She reached for the brocade ribbon.

Molly nodded.

Amie attached it to a pick and tucked it among the hydrangeas at just the right angle.

Molly looked from Amie to the angel to Amie to the basket. "You've got it, kid," she said in awe.

"What?" Amie asked, only half-listening.

Just then Janis walked over. She looked at the arrangement of hydrangeas. "You did better than I expected," she said to Molly. "This is just right."

"Not me," said Molly.

"I did it," said Amie. "Or at least I fixed it."

"She's got it, Mom," said Molly.

"What?" asked Amie.

Janis nodded. "She does."

"What?" asked Amie, by this time irritated.

"The touch. You've got Mom's touch," said Molly. "Where have you been hiding all this talent?"

Amie looked bemused. "You mean fixing stuff like flower arrangements is a talent?"

156

"It's not only the flowers. It's the angel, too. Look, Mom."

Janis studied the little angel and nodded. She looked at Amie and smiled broadly. "You, my dear, are very, very good. Show me what else you've done."

Amie and Janis walked away, leaving Molly smiling to herself. Suddenly Janis was back at her side.

"But don't think this discovery about Amie gets you off the hook."

"I love you, Mom."

Janis shook her head in exasperation and walked back to Amie.

"Look at this, Molly!" Ardith held out a wreath frame on which she was wiring pine cones. "I'm actually making something pretty!"

Molly looked at the wreath and thought pretty might not be the exact word—strange would probably be better, but she'd never say that to Ardith.

"You know what might be a good idea?" Molly asked, trying to think how to be both polite and truthful at the same time. "I think it would be good if all the pine cones sort of faced the same direction instead of racing off in all directions. Sort of like this?" And she realigned a couple of independent thinkers to follow the same pattern.

"I see what you mean," said Ardith. "I can do that."

"And why don't you add about twice as many? You don't want anyone to see the wire frame showing through."

"You don't? Well, okay. There are plenty of pine cones. Did you know your mother has big plastic trash cans full of cones? Each different kind has its own can."

Molly nodded. She remembered more than one family car ride when Janis would suddenly call out, "Stop the car, Ben! There are great pine cones back there! Come on, Molly. Let's get as many as we can."

It might be beech nuts or teasel or milkweed pods instead of pine cones, but the drill was the same. Janis would pull a plastic trash bag out of the box she kept in the trunk for just such an occasion, and they set about filling it up. Until she started junior high school, Molly thought this was what all mothers did.

Suddenly the front doorbell rang.

"I'll get it," yelled Amie, and Molly marveled at her timely recovery from *deafness convenientus*. In no time Amie was back with Suzy, Alyce, and Mary at her side.

"We've got more help for you, Grandmom," she announced grandly. "I asked my friends to come over too, just like Mom did. All you have to do is tell them what to do, and they'll do it."

In the melee that resulted in getting a job for each of the girls, Molly went to Amie.

"Sweetheart, it was nice of you to ask the girls to help, but, really, you should have asked if they could come."

"Yes," said Janis who had materialized at Molly's shoulder, her eyes boring into Molly's. "You should have asked."

Chapter SIXTEEN

Molly sat in her favorite chair in the family room, a swivel rocker she could turn to face the backyard whenever she needed to look upon the constancy—relatively speaking—of the woods. Not that there was much to look at except bare branches this time of year in Pennsylvania, but the beeches and poplars were still strong and tall and solid.

Which was more than relationships with people were. She sighed as she recalled Janis's gimlet stare. Her mother was not happy with her, not by any stretch of the imagination.

"You didn't call ahead, did you?" Sara had asked as they ate the chicken salad and fresh fruit Ardith had provided for lunch. "How come?"

Molly shook her head. "I was afraid to. I knew she'd just say no."

"It'll take her a while to forgive you, I think," Sara said as she watched Janis talk with Amie and the girls. "Even when she decides she's glad you did it, she'll resent it."

Molly nodded glumly. "But I think I'd do it again. I haven't seen her so involved with people or so active for a long time."

When everyone left late in the afternoon, Janis's shelves were full of completed projects and all the work spaces were clean and orderly. Janis thanked everyone most graciously— except Molly.

Now Molly sat in her chair, absently watching Jordan dig in his "cabin" basement again. She smiled in spite of herself. How that boy loved dirt. From the time he was a little guy and dug his first hole, he'd been a dirt freak. For years he wanted to be a ditch digger when he grew up. To be paid for digging in dirt was the greatest thing he could imagine.

His *pièce de résistance* had been the quarry he'd dug three years ago for his Matchbox trucks to work in: a huge, shallow affair with roads and workstations and dumping sites. Now it was a water hole every time it rained, but he couldn't bring himself to fill it in, and he screamed like a wounded animal any time Pete mentioned doing so. He still occasionally repaired the roads in it, and once or twice, when he thought no one was watching, Molly had seen him driving his Matchboxes around its curving streets.

But he had basically decided that he was too old for the quarry, and so he'd moved on to bigger projects like his cabin. His present hole was already five feet square and waist deep. If it got too much deeper, Pete would have to help him shore up the sides. Molly had no desire to look out one day and see him digging himself out.

She squinted as she looked at Jordan. The royal blue sweatshirt he was wearing didn't look familiar. Rather, it did because it was obviously a Remington shirt, but she didn't remember buying him one.

Suddenly, giggles erupted from the direction of Amie's room. Molly spun around as Amie, Suzy, Alyce, and Mary burst into the hall.

"Mom," said Amie, "we're going to go out for dinner and

then maybe go bowling or to a movie or hang out at Suzy's or something."

"Are you asking me or telling me?" Molly said, but with no heat.

All four girls grinned.

"May I?" asked Amie.

"No, no," whispered Suzy dramatically. "It's Simon says, 'May I?'"

Molly laughed with the others. "Who's driving?"

"Me," said Alyce, and Molly's heart rate accelerated. Alyce was a delightful girl, a beautiful girl with black curls and bright blue eyes, but she had the attention span and common sense of a nit. She also had the strange and unnerving habit of talking in italics.

"Well, I'd like Amie home by 11:30, Alyce. Okay?"

It obviously wasn't okay with Amie. "Mom, no one else has a curfew!"

Molly nodded and thought for a minute. Was she asking something too restrictive? She glanced at Alyce, who was rooting madly through her purse for something.

"Look what I *found!*" Alyce cried. She pulled some pictures from the depths of her purse. "I brought them to *show* to you all. They're from the *party* last weekend." She giggled. "I *forgot* I had them."

She handed them to Amie, and Suzy and Mary crowded around.

"You cut off my head," said Suzy.

"More important," said Amie, "she cut off Paul's head. I know he's got a great smile, but it does look best with nose, eyes, and hair above it."

Alyce peered at the pictures. "I *always* cut off heads," she said with sad resignation. "I don't know why. I mean, Paul had a head when I *took* the picture. Why doesn't he have one *in* the picture?"

161

"How come you make the honor roll and yet you can't figure out the simple business of looking through a viewfinder to see how your picture will turn out?"

"I don't *know*," said Alyce seriously. "I sort of *worry* about that." Then she giggled again. "And I can't find the *car keys*."

"They're in your jeans pocket," said Mary. "I saw you put them there."

Alyce looked surprised. She checked and, sure enough, there they were.

And this girl will have Amie's life in her hands, thought Molly. Suddenly she was tempted to forbid the excursion altogether. Instead she said, "11:30, Amie. I mean it."

Amie made a very unladylike face and said with reluctance, "Okay."

"Don't *worry*, Mrs. Gregory," said Alyce. "*I'll* have her home on time."

"And what time is that?" asked Molly, just to see what answer she'd get.

Alyce giggled and looked vacant.

"11:30," said Mary, shaking her head at Alyce.

"Alyce, you do know about stop signs and red lights, don't you?" asked Molly before she could stop herself.

Alyce giggled again. "I passed my test on the *first* try," she said. "*Really*. You don't have to worry."

Somehow Molly wasn't convinced. All she could think of was Sara's comment about the teen years being a mother's great occasion for developing a deep prayer life.

Molly stood in the doorway and watched the girls leave. At the last minute, Amie hurried back and gave her a little hug and a kiss on the cheek. Then she stated the real purpose of her little charade.

"I just want you to know," she said coldly, "that I think the curfew is not only unfair but also unkind."

Molly barely saw Alyce's serpentine exit down the very straight driveway. She was too stunned by Amie's little performance. The story of Judas as performance art, starring Amie Gregory.

So her mother and her daughter were mad at her.

And just think, I made all these enemies trying to be a good person. Makes me wonder what I could do if I tried to make people mad.

She shut the front door in a blue funk.

"I'm not eating dinner here," said P.J. a few minutes later as he emerged from the bathroom wrapped in a towel. "I'm going out with some of the guys."

"Oh?"

"Yes, Grandmom," said P.J. with a grin as he disappeared into his room.

"Oh, dear," said Molly as she heard what she'd said. Not only was everyone mad at her, she was also turning into her mother.

She giggled a bit as she went to the phone and called for a Sicilian pizza to be delivered. She pulled out some paper plates and set them on the table for her and Jordan. When it was almost time for the pizza to arrive, she called to Jordan, who was still outside digging in the meager light from the back door

She was paying the pizza delivery man when Jordan zipped by on his way to his room. A few minutes later he came to the table, hands at least partially clean, white T-shirt beige in numerous places where dirt had seeped through his sweatshirt. He reached for one of the corner pieces of the pizza.

Molly heard a van roar up the drive and beep. She got up and met P.J. as he came from his room. He had Jordan's sweatshirt in his hand.

"Mom," he said seriously as he handed it to her. "I don't think it's very fair of you to buy an expensive sweatshirt like this for Jordan to play in his dirt hole when you won't buy a team jacket for me."

Molly looked at the blue garment with the red RAIDERS emblazoned across the front. She shook her head. "I didn't buy that."

"Then Dad must have. Still unfair." It was obvious P.J. felt somehow the victim of discrimination.

The horn sounded again outside, and P.J. moved toward the door.

"Who are you going out with?" Molly asked.

P.J. shrugged. "Just some of the guys."

"Yes, but who?"

"I won't be too late," P.J. said.

Molly put a hand on his arm. "Who, P.J.? Zack Callender?"

He didn't answer.

"P.J., you know Dad said no."

"I'm just going out with some friends," he said. "What's wrong with that?"

"Where are you going?"

P.J. shrugged. "Around."

"With Zack?"

He pulled the door open.

Molly tightened her hold on his arm. "P.J., there are a few problems here. One, you didn't clear your plans with me. And two, I don't like you driving 'around' with guys two years older than you."

His expression was almost scornful. "For heaven's sake, Mom, two years' age difference isn't a sin."

"Let me finish, please." Molly leaned against the doorjamb. "It's not just his being older. It's his reputation. And Dad's saying no."

The van horn sounded again and a voice yelled, "Come on, P.J.! We're hungry!"

P.J. opened the storm door and waved at his friends to wait. "I've got to go, Mom."

"No, P.J. Not with those guys."

He looked at her, the desire for independence bristling from every pore of his body. Molly felt as if she were looking at a stranger.

Who is this rebellious kid, and what has he done with my P.J.?

"Tell me something, Mom." The chill in his voice was enough to give her pneumonia. "How come you can force your dumb ideas on us whether we like them or not, but I can't even choose my own friends? Isn't it unfair to do things only your way? And don't you owe me? After all, I've been the most cooperative one about this dumb strike thing of yours."

Molly felt as if a main prop had been knocked out from under her and she was in a free fall. "I thought you thought I was right."

He shrugged. "Regardless, you owe me."

Molly shook her head. She knew something was warped in his logic, but she was too distraught to put her finger on what. "No, P.J. I'll never owe you the right to do something we both know is wrong."

Anger at her interference flowed from him like water from a ruptured dam. "I'm not a kid anymore!"

"But you're not a man, either," she said desperately. "I'm still responsible for you whether you like it or not." Suddenly she saw the flaw in his reasoning. "And the reason we do things my way is because I'm the parent. God put me in charge."

"Well, not tonight," he said, pushing the storm door wide. "Not tonight."

"Please, P.J.," she said, grabbing both of his arms.

He looked down at her hands. "Do you really think you can stop me?"

Fighting down panic, Molly looked at her son. She shook

her head. "We both know I can't."

"Well, you're right." He didn't quite sneer. "You can't." And he was out the door, loping across the lawn to the waiting van.

With tears streaming down her face, Molly watched him go. *No, dear God! Please! Don't let him go! Please! Don't let him go!*

As P.J. climbed into the van and it drove away, she sobbed in pain. A huge hand was crushing her ribs and ripping apart her heart.

Oh, God! What do I do now?

Chapter
SEVENTEEN

olly stood there, as though frozen, for a long time. She was afraid to move for fear her legs wouldn't work and she'd fall down.

P.J.! The good kid! The one who read his Bible! The one who supported her strike! What had happened? How had it happened?

Oh, Lord, I'm so scared!

Would he have defied Pete? She didn't think so. There were years of authority and honor there. And there was the physical thing, too. Pete was still bigger than P.J., though not by much, and there was no denying that physical power was something she didn't possess.

She heard the TV come on and she wandered into the family room in a daze. Jordan was being disciplined, and she knew she had to tell him to turn the thing off. But she quite frankly didn't care at the moment.

"Hey, Mom," said Jordan. "There's a really good movie on tonight. I know you'll like it. Not too much blood and guts. It's a comedy and I think..."

His voice trailed away, and he became very still. It took

167

Molly a minute to realize he was staring at her. Or rather at the blue sweatshirt that she still held. His face was taut and what else? Fearful? And there was something about his stillness that wasn't normal.

She looked at the shirt and it finally registered that, though dirty from his excavations, the garment was brand new.

"Jordan," she said, "where did you get this shirt?" She was surprised to hear that her voice barely shook. Maybe she was in shock from Amie's and P.J.'s behavior.

"P.J. gave it to me," the boy said.

Molly shook her head. "No."

"Yes. He knew how much I wanted one, so he used his own food money to buy it for me. Is that a good brother or what?"

Again Molly shook her head. "I know that's not so. Tell me the truth."

"Oh, geez," said Jordan. "Did I say P.J.? I meant Amie. Amie bought it for me."

Molly just looked at him. "You actually expect me to believe that?"

Jordan frowned, obviously scrambling for an answer but drawing a blank.

"So, where did this come from?" Molly held out the sweatshirt. As she did so, she saw a tag still dangling from the inside of the garment. She pulled it out and read aloud, "Mason's. $39.95."

Jordan looked more than a bit scared.

"Mason's," Molly repeated. "Just down the strip mall from the grocery store where you went this morning with P.J." She stared at Jordan in disbelief as she reached the only conclusion possible. "You shoplifted this!"

He harumphed and coughed and fidgeted, but he didn't deny it.

"Jordan!" She heard the shrillness in her voice. *Oh, Lord, please don't let me lose control of myself.* She took several deep breaths. "Whatever possessed you to do such a terrible thing?"

He stared at his feet.

"Jordan. I asked a question that I want answered! Whatever possessed you?"

"It's no big deal, Mom," he said defensively. "It's not like it's something valuable. It's only a sweatshirt."

"Jordan! Of course it's a big deal! You broke the law! You stole something! Jordan, you're a thief." She heard what she said and put her hands to her lips in despair. She whispered, "You're a thief."

He sat up straight, righteous indignation crackling from him. "I am not."

Molly blinked. "Of course you are. You took something that wasn't yours. That makes you a thief."

"No," he said, though a bit uncertainly. "Thieves are scuzzy guys with guns."

"Come on, Jordan! You can't be that naive. A thief is anyone who takes what isn't his." She stared at her youngest. Had she really done such a bad job as a mom that he didn't even know what theft was?

She had a sudden vision of him talking to her on a phone as they sat on either side of a glass panel. Prison guards stood all around, swinging their billy clubs. Other cons sat talking to their molls through glass screens.

Molly shivered. "Don't you realize that if the security people had seen you, I'd be down at the police station bailing you out?"

"Well, they didn't see me." He flopped back in his seat, arms crossed, face belligerent.

"But it's still just as wrong!"

"No," he said firmly. "They didn't see me. It's okay. I didn't get caught."

"Do you honestly think that getting caught is what makes something wrong? You think it's okay to kill someone as long as you don't get caught?"

Jordan squirmed. "Well, no. Killing someone's always wrong."

"And so is taking something that's not yours!" Molly stopped herself from saying more because she was getting shrill again. She closed her eyes to allow herself time to regain control.

Pete! she thought. But he wasn't here. It was just her. And God.

Oh, dear Lord, please give me wisdom and a good idea about how to deal with this. I feel like I'm going crazy!

She stared at Jordan, who looked incredibly young as he slouched in Pete's recliner. "Well, you've got to pay for your crime."

He sat up straight and stared at her. "What do you mean pay? How can I pay? I haven't got that much money."

"You pay by taking the shirt back. We're going down to Mason's right now, and you're going to confess to the manager and ask what you can do to pay for the piece of his property that you stole and then damaged."

Jordan looked appalled. "You're kidding."

"Not in the least. Jordan, I love you too much to let you get away with this."

He stood up abruptly and stared daggers at Molly. "That's the trouble with this family!" he shouted. "There's just too much love!" And he raced to his room and slammed the door.

Molly sat, stunned, and then she began to shake. Her whole body trembled, her teeth chattered, and she was suddenly very cold.

She began to cry.

God, I want to resign. I don't want to be a mom anymore. I want to give them back, all three of them. I'm not strong enough or wise enough to do this right. I want to go to a deserted island all by myself and sleep in the sun until they're twenty-five or thirty years old. Then maybe I'll start talking to them again.

Immediately she felt guilty for such thoughts. She also felt weak and hopeless and defeated. Pete had been gone barely twenty-four hours, and the family was falling apart.

"I'm sorry, dear," she'd say when he came home. "I know that when you left, you had three plain, ordinary, if sloppy, children. It must be a shock to return to a female Judas, a rebel without a cause, and a petty thief. Forgive me?"

Suddenly Mike Schmidt jumped into her lap and began purring. She smiled wanly at him and stroked his soft fur gently.

"I'm glad someone loves me," she told him, sniffling. She kissed him between the ears.

She pulled herself from her chair, the cat in her arms. She turned and put him down on the cushion, petting him as he settled in for a nap. She knew what she had to do.

She felt like an old woman as she walked down the hall to the boys' room. Every step hurt, and it was incredibly difficult to stand erect. She wanted to bend over and cradle her aching heart.

She gave a gentle knock and opened the bedroom door.

Jordan lay on his bed, staring at the ceiling. His jaw was clenched in anger, and he refused to look at her.

"Get your coat, Jordan," she said.

"I'm not going anywhere." He folded his arms across his chest.

Molly walked into the room and stood over him. She looked down at him and said slowly, "Yes, you are. Get your coat."

He stared stonily beyond her, not moving.

And Molly, the woman who hated confrontation, grabbed

him by the front of the shirt and pulled him to his feet. She repeated slowly and distinctly through clenched teeth, her nose mere inches from his, "Get your coat!"

Thoroughly astounded by her show of force, Jordan had his coat on before he realized it. He followed her meekly down the hall.

"Get that sweatshirt," Molly ordered, pointing to where it lay on the family room floor. "Put it in a bag."

"And if I don't want to?" he asked in one last stab at defiance.

"I don't care if you want to," Molly spit. "Put it in a bag!"

Again, astonished, he obeyed.

They arrived at the mall and parked outside Mason's, a small sporting goods store struggling to stay afloat in spite of the Sports Authorities and other superstore chains. It was Mason's ability to provide local school products like the Remington sweatshirt that kept its doors open.

She climbed out of the car. "Come on."

Jordan didn't move.

Molly walked around to the passenger side and opened the door. "Come on."

Jordan wouldn't look at her, and he had a slightly panicky expression on his face.

"Mom, don't make me do this," he said. "Please."

"Sorry, sport. You should have thought about something like this before you acted."

"But this is embarrassing!"

"I certainly hope so," said Molly, who thought it the height of injustice if she were the only one thoroughly humiliated by his actions. She reached in and took the bag containing the sweatshirt from him. "Now come on. Let's go and get it over with."

Sighing deeply, Jordan climbed out of the car. They walked

to Mason's side by side. At the door, Molly held the bag out to Jordan. "It's yours to make right."

They went inside, her stomach in knots. Jordan tried to look nonchalant, but his fear was greater than his acting ability.

"May we see the manager?" asked Molly at the cash register.

"What?" asked the teenager behind the counter.

"The manager. May we see him, please?"

"Do you want to exchange something?" the teen asked, looking at the bag in Jordan's hand. "I can help you with that."

Molly shook her head. "We need to see the manager."

The girl looked uncertainly at Molly, then said, "Just a minute." She disappeared into the back of the store and returned in a few minutes with a tired-looking man wearing a very wrinkled shirt that hung out of his pants in the back. He walked as though his feet hurt, and he'd obviously had a very long, hard day.

"I'm Molly Gregory," Molly said. "This is my son Jordan. He has something to tell you."

The man looked at Jordan and waited. There was no curiosity in him, and Molly realized he knew what was coming. How many other times had he listened to kids confess?

"I took this," said Jordan, staring at his feet as he held out the bag.

The man took the bag and peered in. He showed no emotion and said nothing.

"And," prompted Molly.

"And I want to know what I can do to pay for it since I don't have any money," Jordan said miserably

"You can stay out of my store," said the man quickly but without rancor, as if he were too weary to get mad. "I'm so tired of you kids coming in here and stealing stuff. You think you're so clever, like I don't know. Well, I don't want you in here ever again. You or your friends. All the time stealing me blind."

"I never took anything before," Jordan said, taken aback by the accusations. "Honest."

"Oh, sure," said the man. "Like you expect me to believe that?"

"It's true," said Jordan. "And I'm sorry I took this shirt. I really am. Please let me pay it off somehow."

The man shook his head. "Just leave and never come back." He turned from Jordan to Molly. "And you, Mother. I can see you've been crying."

Jordan looked at Molly in surprise. He hadn't noticed her red, puffy eyes before.

The man continued. "At least you tried—which is better than most parents these days. You look like a nice lady. I hope you don't have to visit this little thief in jail someday."

He turned back to stare at Jordan. "Which you will if he ever comes into this store again." And he turned and walked tiredly back to his office, the bag with the sweatshirt dangling from his hand.

Jordan stared after the man, poleaxed. People always believed him. People always thought he was cute and clever. No one but Amie had ever talked to him like that man had, and Amie didn't really count.

Molly touched his arm and turned toward the door. Her eye caught that of the young cashier, who was smiling broadly at Jordan, enjoying his discomfiture. When she realized Molly was watching her, she killed the smile, but her eyes were still dancing.

A stab of pure pain ripped through Molly. It was her son the girl was laughing at!

"Mom," said Jordan when they were back in the car. "He didn't believe me! He thought I came in there before and took stuff. He thought I'd come in there again and take stuff!"

"Did you? Would you?" Molly asked.

"Mom!" Jordan was clearly hurt. "Don't you believe me either?"

"What do you expect, Jordan?"

"I thought I could at least count on you."

"Honey, thieves are not the most trustworthy people, and you aligned yourself with that group when you took that shirt. How do I know I can trust you now?"

"But you've known me all my life!"

"And I never would have believed you would do something like you did. I feel betrayed, Jordan."

He was silent for a minute, frowning as he struggled to understand what was happening. Suddenly he said, "Are you going to tell Dad?"

Molly nodded. "We don't keep secrets from each other."

"Don't tell him, Mom. Please!"

"Why not?"

"Because he'll think I'm terrible." Jordan looked at her with sad eyes.

"You should have thought about all the implications before you acted, kiddo."

"Are you going to tell P.J. and Amie, or Grandmom and Pop-pop and Mom-mom?"

Molly could see the tension in every line of his body. "I don't see any reason that they need to know—*if* you keep your nose clean."

He nodded miserably. "Don't worry. I will."

Dear Lord, prayed Molly, *please let that be the truth!*

Chapter EIGHTEEN

Molly sat in the darkened living room for a long time, alternately praying and worrying. They hardly used this room since they'd added the family room to the back of the house a few years ago. But it felt right to come into the room they had lived in when the kids were small and their problems were small. Maybe the memories of happier days would help her tonight.

Jordan was back in his room reading or sleeping or something. Had he learned his lesson? With all that natural curiosity he possessed, how could she and Pete possibly keep him from getting into trouble until he reached adulthood? Maybe the neighbors wouldn't notice if they put iron bars on his windows. Or maybe all she needed were handcuffs to attach him to his bed for the next ten years.

And Amie! Would she come home by curfew or would there be another confrontation? How could they ever get her to think more of other people than herself, to respect her mother, to speak kindly? It was probably too late for washing her mouth out with soap—even if people actually did that in real life, which Molly doubted.

And P.J.! Molly's heart lurched. Where was he and what trouble was he up to? How had he gone from good kid to outright rebel in less than two weeks? Was it her fault because she went on the strike? If she were still driving him...

Oh, God, how do any kids ever reach maturity without killing themselves or their parents? I'm absolutely scared to death! I can't do this! You said when I'm weak, you're strong. Well, I'm weak. Please be strong for me!

She thought of a bumper sticker she'd read last week: "Raising kids is like being nibbled to death by a duck." Tonight it felt more like being swallowed whole by Jonah's whale.

When the phone rang, shattering the silence, Molly jumped so wildly that she banged her hand against the corner of the end table. Shaking it to get rid of the pain, she hurried to answer, glancing at the clock. 11:05.

Dread filled her, and her heart beat so fast it hurt. It was a rule: no good ever came of a phone call after ten o'clock at night.

"Hello?" she said breathlessly.

"Mom! Help me!" a voice whispered.

Molly felt as though she had slammed into a wall. "P.J.? What's wrong?"

"Just come!"

"Where?"

"The Turkey Hill mini-mart and gas station at Price and Waterford."

"I'm on my way."

Without hesitation she grabbed her coat and purse, called to Jordan that she'd be right back, and tore out of the house. She'd never driven so recklessly or so fast. She wasn't even sure if she drew a single breath during the whole, horrible trip. Her shoulders were so tight with nerves and fear that they were practically at ear level. She screeched into the parking lot and hit the brakes.

Whatever she had expected—and she really had no idea what that was—she didn't find. Everything looked normal. There were several cars parked in front of the store, several people inside getting milk or bread or renting a last minute movie, several vehicles at the gas pumps.

She climbed hesitantly from the car, disoriented, trying to adjust from the terror of the trip to the ordinariness of the Turkey Hill. Had she imagined P.J.'s call?

Mom! Help me!

No. That had been real. She just didn't understand what was going on yet. Or—maybe she was too late!

She looked wildly around the parking lot for P.J. but didn't see him. She rushed into the store and circled the interior. Still she didn't see him. She went to the checkout counter.

"Did you see—" she was asking, when suddenly the door opened and a bunch of high school guys tumbled in.

"Thash ten dollars on number four," said a tall, husky, handsome kid, offering a bill to pay for his gas over Molly's shoulder. As Molly turned to look at him, he belched and grinned.

"Shorry," he mumbled with a charming grin. As his breath rippled across the space between them, the alcohol fumes caught in Molly's throat.

"Hey, Zack," called a skinny boy over in the snack aisle. "Corn chips or potato chips?"

"How about both?" the boy next to Molly yelled back. "And some dip and some salsa."

Molly stepped back a bit, both to focus better and to avoid the fumes. There was a lot written about secondhand smoke. What about secondhand alcohol? Was there such a thing?

"Are you Zack Callender?" she asked.

He squinted at her and nodded.

"I'm P.J. and Amie Gregory's mother." She stuck out her hand.

He looked her up and down rather insolently and grinned. "Hi." He ignored her hand.

The door opened again and three girls and P.J. came in. Two of the girls were hanging all over him, their arms wrapped around him as though they couldn't stand without his support. The third was flashing a beautiful set of teeth at him while her fingers twirled coyly in her long blond hair.

Molly watched the performance sourly, wondering how much the orthodontist's bill had been and what brand of dye the blond was. This was what she had almost killed herself to see?

"Hello, P.J.," she said, her voice abrupt with annoyance. He had issued this plea for help, causing her to risk life and limb, and here he was, ladies' man of the hour. What gall!

"Mom!" said P.J. with great surprise. "What in the world are you doing here?"

Molly blinked. "You ca—" She stopped as she caught the slight shake of his head. She began again. "Milk. I need some milk for tomorrow. So we can have a good breakfast before we go to Sunday school and church." She took special care to speak slowly and emphasize *Sunday school* and *church,* and she knew the last sentence wasn't the evil twin but her own anger speaking.

P.J. slowly disengaged himself from his fan club and introduced the girls as Bambi, Heather, and Amber.

Perfect names for a trio of sweet young things on the prowl, Molly thought unkindly.

"Let me just help my mom get her milk," he said to the girls as if Molly were ninety-five years old and counting. He took her by the arm and walked with her to the milk aisle, smiling jauntily. He glanced casually back over his shoulder.

Suddenly he dropped the cool guy facade, bent, and whispered desperately, "Get me out of here!"

She looked at him thoughtfully. Why, besides transportation home, did he need her help? "What's your plan? We run out the front door, jump in the car, and burn rubber? You make it sound like you're being held against your wishes or something."

He waved away her absurd comments. "I thought maybe you could plead fear because Dad's away, and I'd have to take you home to calm you down."

"I'm supposed to cry and whimper and cling? Is that what you mean?"

He nodded.

She crossed her arms and stared at him coldly. He looked uncomfortable under her gaze and at least had the grace to blush.

"Let me get this straight," she said. *God, please give me the right words here!* "You want me to act the idiot so you can be the hero. That way you get out of what is obviously a very bad situation—I take it Zack is driving?"

P.J. nodded.

"I thought so—and your reputation as a cool kid will still be intact."

"Well." He squirmed. "Yes."

"P.J., obviously I don't want you driving off with a guy already half looped, but I don't want to lie either."

"You don't have to lie," he said eagerly. "Just hang on to me like you're really upset, and I'll take care of the rest."

"In other words, you'll lie."

That stopped him.

"Hey, P.J.," called a high, girl-woman's voice from the end of the aisle. P.J. and Molly turned to find the blond Amber being ambidextrous as she twirled her hair with one hand and waved two fingers at him with the other. "Zack wants to leave." She paused and breathed deeply, her chest rising and falling with great charm. "Me, too." Her smile was full of meaning.

"In a minute," P.J. said, jerking his head slightly to indicate Molly.

Amber moved away, and Molly turned to P.J.

"I didn't realize you were such a phony," she said. "I thought you really did love the Lord. I thought you really were a good kid! I believed your act! What an idiot I am!"

He grabbed her arm, hurt in his face. "I *do* love the Lord. I *am* a good kid. That's why I want out!"

"Then get out honorably, P.J." Her voice quivered with intensity. "Don't hide behind me. Stand up for what you believe. Be more interested in making the Lord pleased than Zack or Amber or any of those kids."

She watched the emotions roll across his face as he struggled with what to do.

Dear God, help him!

"P.J., when Dad and I became Christians, it meant making choices we'd never had to make before. We lost some friends who suddenly found us too 'good' for them."

P.J. nodded, not looking terribly impressed but still listening. Somehow, Molly knew, parents' stories never touched the pain of the present generation's circumstances. It was truly every man for himself. But she kept trying.

"There's a cost to following Jesus that you haven't had to pay before," she said. "You've been such a natural leader and such a fun guy that the kids accepted you and liked you in spite of your squeaky-clean style. Tonight is choice time, honey, and I can't make that choice for you. All I can do is pray that you've got the courage I always thought you had."

She turned and walked up the aisle, a half-gallon of milk cradled in her arms like a baby.

Oh God, oh God, oh God, was all she could articulate. In those two words were all her hopes and dreams and prayers for this most gifted of kids. *Oh God, oh God, oh God!*

She took her place in line at the cash register. When she looked out the front windows, she could see Zack and Amber and several kids standing around a van, waiting for P.J. One of the boys reached in the van and pulled out a six pack. He gave a can to Zack and another to Amber, pulled one off the plastic restraints for himself and gave the other three to another boy who took one and passed it on. Eventually the plastic holder was tossed in the general direction of the trash bin.

The cans did not hold soda.

Oh God, oh God, oh God!

She finished paying for her unnecessary milk at the same time P.J. reappeared from the milk aisle. He patted her on the arm as he walked past and outside. He turned toward the van.

Oh God, oh God, oh God!

She caught the door as it swung shut and went to stand at the curb. She would throw herself in front of the van if need be to keep it from leaving with PJ inside, but not yet. P.J. needed his chance.

"Come on, P.J.," said Amber, leeching on to him. "I've got something special for you inside."

The boys all hooted and snickered. The skinny one reached in the van and pulled out another six pack. He pulled off a can and held it out to P.J.

Oh God, oh God, oh God! Molly's heart was about to jump out of her chest—which was probably why she couldn't breathe.

P.J. shook his head at the boy with the can. He took Amber by the hand and peeled her loose, then turned to Zack.

"I'm not going, Zack. I can't."

There was a momentary silence. Then Amber looked over at Molly with narrowed, spiteful eyes. "I didn't know," she said to P.J. in tones that dripped venom, "that you were a mama's boy."

P.J. glanced at Molly and smiled briefly. "I'm not," he told

Amber. "But I had temporarily forgotten Whose boy I was. Now I know."

Zack spit in disgust, the ball of phlegm landing on the edge of P.J.'s gym shoe. He smirked in satisfaction, then leaned into P.J.'s face and called him name after name, his anger ugly and unwarranted.

P.J. stood quietly through it all, and Molly's heart broke for him.

"In the van, everyone," Zack finally ordered. "I should have known better than to try and make something out of someone like him."

As the doors slammed shut, P.J. turned to walk toward Molly. His face looked sickly in the parking lot lights, but there was a strength and pride there that delighted her.

Thank you, thank you, thank you! was all she could think. Trying to act in a way that wouldn't embarrass him—she was certain throwing her arms around his neck and bursting into tears or dancing for joy across the parking lot would seem inappropriate—Molly walked toward the car with P. J. beside her. She heard the van tear out of the lot, and she glanced up to see it run the stop sign at the corner just as a patrol car turned into Turkey Hill.

With a squeal of the patrol car's tires, the chase was on.

Molly leaned weakly against the car. If P.J. had chosen differently, he would have been in that van, in that chase. With hands that didn't work quite right, she fumbled the door open and the key into the ignition.

Then she sat still. She didn't trust herself to drive.

"Want to tell me about the evening?" she asked.

P.J. did. He needed to talk.

"We went to Pizzano's Pizza for dinner. The guys tried to get beer, but they were carded and didn't get served. We all laughed about it, and I told myself they were just trying to be funny. Then we went to the movies, to the 8:30 show. Amie was there with Mary, Alyce, and Suzy. Zack and the guys made lots of rude comments about them, especially about how snotty and holier-than-thou they were."

He was silent for a minute, remembering. He looked at Molly. "I don't think the girls heard, but—" He stopped again and swallowed hard. "Mom, I didn't even stand up for my own sister, let alone her friends."

"Amie can seem a little stiff and unapproachable if she doesn't like someone," Molly said, trying to give him some slack.

He shook his head. "You don't know how hard it is to be a 'good' kid. Guys like Zack can make your life miserable. They mock you all the time for not playing around with sex or drinking or doing drugs. I should have been singing Amie's praises, not laughing along with those goons. I was awful, Mom. I can't believe I was so awful."

Molly patted his hand. "Like you said, it's hard."

"Don't be so nice to me, Mom. I don't deserve it."

They drove home at a far more leisurely pace than Molly had come. P.J. kept talking.

"After the movie was over, Zack found some guy to go get beer and scotch for us. We'd already picked up Amber and Heather and Bambi at the movies. Or they picked us up; I'm not sure which. We started just driving around, drinking. I was getting more and more scared, but I didn't know what to do." He looked away, out the far window. His voice was soft as if he hated to admit what he needed to say. "I was in way over my head and I knew it, but I didn't want them to think I wasn't cool. So I pretended I was drinking, too."

Molly's heart broke for him. He had always been so wise, so able to make good choices. The memory of this evening would eat at him for a long, long time.

185

He turned back to her. "We needed gas, so Zack pulled into the Turkey Hill lot. I pleaded bathroom and ran. I found the phone and called. My biggest fear was that they'd see me and ask what I was doing. I don't know what I'd have told them, but I'd have lied." He smiled sadly. "But then, you already know that."

After a few miles of silence he said, "I have to apologize for the way I acted when I left and for asking you to bail me out. I put you in a terrible position. I didn't realize I was such a coward."

"Your apology is accepted, P.J. But don't be too hard on yourself. You behaved like anything but a coward there at the end. Everything turned out okay. Thank God for that, rather than wasting time berating yourself."

When they finally turned into the driveway, Molly breathed a great sigh. Safe at home!

Chapter NINETEEN

The living room lights were on when they pulled into the garage, and the door flew open before they stopped. Jordan stood there in his pajamas, feet apart, hair wild.

"What's wrong?" he called. "What happened? Why'd you have to run out in the middle of the night?"

"She had to rescue me, kid," said P.J. as he climbed from the car. He reached back in for the milk. "But everything's fine."

Jordan sagged in relief. "I was afraid somebody called and said Dad had a heart attack or something."

"Oh, honey, I'm sorry. I didn't mean to scare you." Molly hugged the boy, ashamed she hadn't thought he'd worry. He must have been distressed because he hugged her back. She released him, giving him a quick kiss on the cheek, and he didn't even protest.

Molly smiled at him. "We're all fine. And Dad's fine. At least I'm assuming he is, since we haven't heard from him because he arrived at camp yesterday. He's too busy growing his beard to call home."

"Beard?" said Jordan with a look of amazement. "Dad's growing a beard?"

"At least for two days," Molly said. She made a face. "Just long enough to be very prickly."

"If you say so, Mom," said Jordan with a significant look. "I wouldn't know about things like that."

Finally, knowing she could avoid the question no longer, Molly asked, "Is Amie home?"

Jordan shook his head. "No."

She slid up her sleeve to check her watch and sighed. "11:45. She's late."

"Don't worry, Mom," said P.J. "She'll be here soon. You know how those girls can be."

"Yeah, sure," said Molly, adding, "Alyce is driving."

"Oh, boy," said Jordan. "The ditz. They're all probably in a ditch somewhere."

"Jordan," hissed P.J. "Watch what you say!"

Jordan looked, wide-eyed and repentant, at Molly. "I was just making a joke, Mom. A very bad joke. I'm sorry. Alyce is a fine driver."

Suddenly Molly felt utterly weary. She couldn't remember ever feeling so tired. The adrenaline rush of the past half-hour was gone, and the lethargy that follows such an outpouring had hit full force.

I'm a limp dishrag afloat on the sea of life, and I'm about to sink under the weight of it all, she thought melodramatically. *God, I don't think I can go through another emotional cataclysm tonight! You're going to have to do it for me.*

The boys came and sat with Molly in the living room, apparently thinking she either needed company or shouldn't be left alone. They said nothing, just kept looking at her, then at each other. Finally she could take their concern no longer.

"You can go to your room, guys. I think I'd rather wait by myself."

"Really?" The relief in Jordan's voice was almost comical. He and P.J. disappeared down the hall.

At midnight Molly wandered into the family room and turned on the TV—at least the noise would fill the emptiness. P.J., who had apparently heard the sound, reappeared and sat in Pete's recliner with Mike Schmidt in his lap and watched the late movie with only an occasional glance at Molly. The Cheshire Cat curled his orange body around Molly's ankles and waited, too.

At 12:15 a car zoomed up the drive. Molly got to her feet slowly. Another confrontation. Another call for wisdom and the right words. Not that she cared anymore. She was just about nibbled to death.

God, I don't think I can do this.

P.J. stood beside her as if to give her strength.

Car doors slammed and voices called, "Come on! Hurry!" People raced across the lawn and burst through the front door.

"Mom! Mom!" It was Amie, her voice raw with panic and fear. "Where are you?"

Molly and P.J. looked at each other, startled. Whatever they had expected from Amie, this wasn't it.

"I'm in here," Molly called.

Amie surged into the room with Mary, Suzy, and Alyce hard on her heels. All four had been crying.

"Where's P.J., Mom?" Amie sobbed. "Where is he?"

Suddenly she saw her brother standing, more than slightly astonished by his sister's emotional excesses, in the middle of the room. She froze.

"P.J.!" she screamed with great joy, and threw her arms around him. "It's P.J.! He's okay! He's okay!"

Mary, Suzy, and Alyce grabbed him too, jumping up and down and hugging him and patting him on the back and even giving him a kiss or two. All four of the girls started crying all over again.

"Oh, thank you, God!" said Amie to the ceiling. "Thank you!" And she kissed P.J. squarely between the eyes.

P.J., totally overwhelmed, tried to pull himself free without much success.

"Oh, Mrs. Gregory, we were so *scared!*" It was Alyce, finally releasing P.J. and turning to the stunned Molly. "When we saw that *van!*"

Molly and P.J. looked at each other immediately, fearful of what they could already guess had happened.

"What van?" asked P.J.

"Zack's," said Alyce.

"Where?"

"Over on Zimmer *Road.* It's on the way from *my* house to here, you know." Alyce looked at Molly with the explanation. "It's why we're so *late.* We *would* have been on time."

"Accident?" asked P.J., Amie still draped around his neck.

Alyce turned back to him and nodded. "Bad."

Amie agreed. "Very bad." She looked at Molly. "We would have been on time, Mom. We left Alyce's at 11:15. Plenty of time."

All three girls nodded. "Plenty of time," they agreed.

"But we got stopped because this accident had just happened. The cops made us pull over to the side of the road and wait while all the emergency vehicles went by. And then the ambulances started coming."

"You wouldn't *believe* it, Mrs. Gregory," said Alyce. "They just kept coming and *coming.*"

Amie nodded. "It was unbelievable, Mom. There were so many! We waited and waited. Then they finally let us drive by, and we saw the van."

She started blinking back new tears. "It was Zack's! And we knew P.J. had been with him because we saw them together at the movies! I thought I'd die on the spot!" She sniffled and kissed P.J. on the cheek, a loud smooch. He hugged her back.

"We *stopped* and asked what *happened*," said Alyce. "But the cop didn't know much. 'I'm just directing *traffic*, lady,' he said. 'And you got to keep *moving*.'" She smiled. "He called me lady."

"I think he knew what had happened all right but just wouldn't tell," said Mary cynically.

"I don't blame him," said Suzy. "By that time we were all crying and screaming and asking if P.J. had been in the accident. All the man wanted to do was get rid of us."

"I kept yelling, 'But my brother might have been in that car! My brother!' But he wouldn't listen," said Amie. "I felt so helpless!"

"He told us to go *home* and talk to our *parents*," said Alyce. "If P.J. had been in there, he said, *you'd* know."

Molly thought of the van going through the stop sign and the patrol car chasing after it. P.J. had come so close to being in it. She thought of Amie's scare and Jordan's sweatshirt and the charming drunk who swore unconscionably at P.J., and her knees just gave way. She sat abruptly on the floor.

"Thank you, God, that my children are all safe with me," she whispered.

Sunday after church Molly and the kids stopped at the hospital to find out how Zack, Amber, and the others were doing. An early morning phone call hadn't yielded much information beyond learning that all were alive.

To their surprise, they were able to visit with Amber, who, beyond a broken arm, wasn't badly hurt. "She's not had anyone come in to see her so far," said the floor nurse. "It'll be good for her to have some visitors."

"No one?" said Molly.

The nurse just shook her head at the sad situation. "All the other young fools have had family here all night. But not Amber." She shrugged. "I don't know why."

They walked awkwardly into the room where Amber lay, half asleep. She slowly opened her eyes, and when she saw P.J. and Molly, tried to pull herself into a sitting position.

"Hey, Amber," said P.J.

"What are you doing here?" she asked, clearly surprised. "I never thought I'd see you again. Ever. Or maybe I never thought you'd want to see me again. Ever."

"We wanted to be sure you were okay." P.J. walked to the bed. "Are you?"

Amber tried to shrug, but flinched in obvious pain. She cradled her injured arm in its bulky dressings. After a minute she said without conviction, "I'm okay, I guess. I'm better off than the others, anyway."

There was an awkward silence, and not knowing what else to say, P.J. fell back on custom. "This is my mom." He indicated Molly.

"Yeah, I know," said Amber, looking embarrassed.

"And this is my brother and sister. Amie saw the wreck."

"You saw it happen?" Amber asked, amazed. "You saw the whole thing?"

Amie shook her head. "I saw it afterwards. It was awful!" She shivered and hugged herself. "I thought P.J. was in there."

Molly put her arm around Amie's waist.

Amie glanced at her and smiled, then turned back to Amber. "You're lucky to be alive, you know. Any of you. It was..." Words failed her.

Amber nodded, looking haunted. "I know. It was so bad! You can't believe how bad. I was so scared. Zack was driving like a maniac. And the cops kept coming and coming, and Zack kept trying to outrun them. Everyone was screaming and falling all over the place, because none of us had seat belts on.

I'm not hurt worse because I'd just fallen off my seat onto the floor."

Molly listened to Amber's tale in a kind of amazed pity. But the most amazing thing was that somehow the girl managed to look beautiful even with a black eye and matted, dirty hair and wearing a hospital gown. All her coyness was gone, knocked out of her over on Zimmer Road, and what remained had more substance than Molly would have imagined.

"When Zack went off the road," Amber continued, staring blindly at her memories, "he crashed into that tree. I was on the floor, wedged between the seats, and didn't go flying like the others. But I've never been so scared in my life, especially when Mick landed on top of me and kept bleeding and bleeding in my face." She looked at P.J. with tragic eyes. "I didn't know we had so much blood in us."

P.J. reached out for her hand. "Shh," he said softly. "You'll be all right. It'll be all right."

Her eyes filled with tears. "I just wish I had a mom who cared enough to come looking for me."

Oh no, Lord, thought Molly. *How do I dislike a girl who gives me a backhanded compliment like that? And where, by the way, is her mother?*

P.J. patted Amber's hand a few more times while she smiled weakly and oh-so-beautifully at him.

Molly sighed as she watched her son fall for the girl like the proverbial ton of bricks. Every latent chivalrous gene in his system leaped into action when she looked at him like that. Even Jordan looked bowled over.

Dear Lord, we're going to need you a lot in the near future. I can see it coming.

Soon even P.J.'s company couldn't keep Amber from succumbing to her pain medicine, and they left so she could sleep.

"Don't look so lost, P.J.," said Amie with more than a touch of vinegar. "You can come see her again."

"Don't worry about the others," a nurse told them. "They're hurt in varying degrees, but they'll be all right in time. However, I don't think the big one is going to be wrestling anytime soon. Two broken legs."

Molly drove the kids from the hospital to Janis's. *Another emotional wringer coming right up,* she thought.

"Hey, Mom," she said warily as the kids bore Trojan away or vice versa.

"Molly," said Janis without any apparent rancor.

Greatly encouraged, Molly said what was on her heart. "Are you still mad at me for bringing everybody over yesterday?"

Janis shrugged. "I spent all last night and this morning fuming, but I do see that you were trying to be helpful. I guess I forget that these last few months have been difficult for you, too."

Molly blinked back her tears as she hugged her mother.

"Anyway," said Janis, taking a big breath. "I've decided to have the Christmas Cupboard—"

"Yes!" said Molly.

"But this will be the last year."

"What? Why?" Molly felt punch-drunk. Janis was giving with one hand and taking with the other. But there was a whole year to get her to change her mind.

"I've decided that I've got to keep myself busier, get out of the house more."

Molly nodded as if this were a new idea. "Do you think so?"

"And so I've decided to open a shop. After all, people have been asking for my things to be available all year for a long time."

Molly stared at her mother. "A shop? You want to open a shop? What a wonderful idea!"

"And I'd like to ask you to be my partner in this operation,

194

if you think you can put up with your mother as a partner. If I understood Pete right when he went over my money with me last weekend, I think I've got enough to get something going. And there's always the bank. I do have a good reputation as a producer of salable goods, so I think they'd give me a loan if I needed one."

Molly was overwhelmed. "It sounds great, Mom. Having the shop, I mean. And maybe I'll be your partner." Visions of Sherm and Pete danced before her. "I just need to think about it and pray about it since it's such a new idea and such a big commitment. I've only been thinking of consignment shops, not having one of my own. Our own."

"It is a big decision," Janis agreed. "Take your time. I don't need to know until after Christmas."

This has been a day portending future adventures, Molly thought as they finally pulled into their own garage. *I think I should feel more nervous than I do.*

"Hey, Dad's home," shouted Jordan when he saw the second car in the garage.

Molly's heart gave a little flutter. It would be wonderful to have him back again.

Jordan threw open the door to the house. "Dad! Wait—" He stopped dead still, a look of wonder on his face. He turned back to Molly. "I smell roast beef! Mom, you've got me salivating like that Russian guy's dogs."

"Mom," said PJ. hopefully. "You shouldn't have."

"Don't get your hopes up," said Amie. "She didn't. It's not for us. We've got three more days left on her strike."

Molly smiled. "We do, but I did. When I stuck the food in the Crock Pot before we left for church this morning, I figured that after last night, we needed some family time around the table. Think of all we've got to tell Dad."

"What have you got to tell Dad?" Pete asked as he came into the room. He hugged the kids and then turned to Molly. He wrapped his arms around her, and for a minute she just delighted in his touch. Then she smelled a grand spicy lime fragrance and stepped back. She reached up and stroked his cheek.

"You just shaved," she said, smiling.

He smiled back and raised one eyebrow. She blushed.

"So what do you have to tell me?" he asked again, his arm draped over Molly's shoulders.

"Well," said Jordan as he tried to see through the condensation on the lid of the Crock Pot. "We need to tell you that Mom's one tough lady."

"Really?" said Molly. "I'm a tough lady?"

"Among the toughest," said P.J. as he gave her a hug.

Molly preened. "Why, that's one of the nicest things anyone's ever said to me." She hugged the comment to herself for a few minutes. "And now I've got something nice to tell you guys."

They all looked at her expectantly.

"I've been thinking that we need to have a family meeting tonight after dinner. It's time to give real life a try again."

The kids looked at each other with delight.

"Like you're going to cook for us again and do all the other stuff?" asked Jordan. "Like life's returning to normal?"

Molly shrugged. "It depends on how we define normal these days. I think we need to talk about things, maybe draw up a family contract."

"And if we do, you'll cook?" pursued Jordan.

Molly nodded. "Not if. When. *When* we do, we'll give real life a try again."

"Whatever you say, Mom," said Amie.

"Whatever," said P.J.

"Yeah, whatever," agreed Jordan.

Molly smiled at Pete. The sweet music of family.

GREGORY FAMILY CONTRACT

I. Our Principles

  A. Because this is our home, its care and keeping are our responsibility.

  B. Our home will be based on Christian principles.

    1. Parents: "These commandments that I give you today are to be upon your hearts. Impress them on your children. Talk about them when you sit at home and when you walk along the road, when you lie down and when you get up" (Deut.6:6–7).

    2. Children: "Children, obey your parents in the Lord, for this is right. 'Honor your father and mother'— which is the first commandment with a promise— 'that it may go well with you and that you may enjoy long life on the earth'" (Eph.6:1–3).

    3. In accordance with Scripture, the parents have the last word, though the children's views will be listened to and carefully considered.

II. Our Patterns

  A. General responsibilities

    1. Each person will keep his or her bedroom or part

thereof clean and ordered. Weekly checks will be made.

2. Each person will hang up and put away his or her own clothes.
3. Each person will dispose of his or her snack mess.
4. Each person will clean up his or her own bathroom debris and dirt.
5. Each person will put away all his or her belongings daily.
   a. Any items left in the public part of the house at bedtime will go in the Dump Box.
   b. Items may be retrieved from the Dump Box upon payment of a twenty-five cent fine per item.
   c. All monies collected will go into a fund to take the family out to dinner.

B. Specific Responsibilities
   1. Dad
      a. will oversee upkeep and repairs about the house.
      b. will spend time with each and all of us.
      c. will take one kid per month out to dinner at a restaurant (reasonable) of the kid's choice.
   2. Mom
      a. will buy food and provide meals.
         1. To be served at 7:00 a.m., 12:00 p.m., and 6:30
         2. All are expected to be present unless stated in advance.
         3. Guests are welcome with prior notice.
         4. Those absent without notice won't eat.
      b. will oversee housekeeping tasks.
      c. will oversee chauffeur services—twenty-four hour advance notice is requested.
      d. will do family laundry.
         1. All dirty clothes are kept in hampers.

2. Each person must bring his or her own clothes to the laundry room on laundry day and return them to their room after wash.

   e. will continue to develop and market needlework.

3. Amie

   a. will care for the living room and dining room—sweeping and dusting twice weekly.

   b. will be responsible for the sewing and maintenance of her wardrobe.

   c. will help with the preparation of dinner.

   d. will make her own lunches.

   e. will fold her laundered clothes.

4. P.J.

   a. will care for the family room—sweeping, dusting, and tidying as needed.

   b. will care for the cats.

     1. Feed and water daily.

     2. Change litter boxes weekly.

   c. will oversee Dump Box and fines

   d. will make his own lunches.

   e. will fold his laundered clothes.

5. Jordan

   a. will collect newspapers and empty the kitchen trash daily.

   b. will take all trash down for collection weekly.

   c. will carry in the groceries.

   d. will make his own lunches.

   e. will fold his laundered clothes.

C. Rotating Responsibilities of Children:
Setting and clearing the table and loading the dish washer will be done monthly on a rotating basis.

D. Seasonal Responsibilities of Children:
Seasonal chores like mowing the grass, shoveling the

walk and drive, and raking the leaves will be assigned by the parents and are viewed as opportunities to earn extra spending money.

NOTE: Failure to comply with these patterns may result in:
1. curtailment of allowance.
2. suspension of social or special privileges such as driving.
3. other disciplines as necessary.

Signed:

Dear Reader,

I remember very clearly how tough it was raising our two boys, now both young, married family men. My husband Chuck and I talked long and hard about what our patterns for our home would be. We dissected our parents' methods. We read books. We watched and listened. We talked with other parents.

But we always remembered one principle: God gave the authority in the home to the parents, not to the children. It is the parents' responsibility to open doors of opportunity and set boundaries beyond which the children may not go.

As God, the Perfect Parent, doesn't say yes to all our whims, neither should we to our kids. As God will go toe-to toe with us when we disobey, so must we face necessary confrontations. But God also always listens; God always has time for us. God always loves us and forgives us.

Through prayer (lots of it!), searching of Scriptures, assessing the abilities and gifts of each child and spending great quantities of time with each one, parents guide and train. Chores like in the Gregory Family Contract (which is modeled after the Roper Family Contract) are just one part of a healthy growing-up, along with laughter and serious talks and vacations and summer jobs and the frequent, firm no at the candy counter.

PALISADES...PURE ROMANCE

～ PALISADES ～

Reunion, Karen Ball
Refuge, Lisa Tawn Bergren
Torchlight, Lisa Tawn Bergren
Treasure, Lisa Tawn Bergren
Chosen, Lisa Tawn Bergren
Firestorm, Lisa Tawn Bergren
Surrender, Lynn Bulock
Wise Man's House, Melody Carlson
Arabian Winds, Linda Chaikin
Lions of the Desert, Linda Chaikin
Cherish, Constance Colson
Chase the Dream, Constance Colson
Angel Valley, Peggy Darty
Sundance, Peggy Darty
Moonglow, Peggy Darty
Promises, Peggy Darty (September, 1997)
Love Song, Sharon Gillenwater
Antiques, Sharon Gillenwater
Song of the Highlands, Sharon Gillenwater
Texas Tender, Sharon Gillenwater
Secrets, Robin Jones Gunn
Whispers, Robin Jones Gunn
Echoes, Robin Jones Gunn
Sunsets, Robin Jones Gunn
Clouds, Robin Jones Gunn
Coming Home, Barbara Jean Hicks
Snow Swan, Barbara Jean Hicks
Irish Eyes, Annie Jones
Father by Faith, Annie Jones (September, 1997)

Glory, Marilyn Kok
Sierra, Shari MacDonald
Forget-Me-Not, Shari MacDonald
Diamonds, Shari MacDonald
Stardust, Shari MacDonald
Westward, Amanda MacLean
Stonehaven, Amanda MacLean
Everlasting, Amanda MacLean
Promise Me the Dawn, Amanda MacLean
Kingdom Come, Amanda MacLean
Betrayed, Lorena McCourtney
Escape, Lorena McCourtney
Dear Silver, Lorena McCourtney
Enough! Gayle Roper
Voyage, Elaine Schulte

⤳ ANTHOLOGIES ⤲
A Christmas Joy, Darty, Gillenwater, MacLean
Mistletoe, Ball, Hicks, McCourtney
A Mother's Love, Bergren, Colson, MacLean
Silver Bells, Bergren, Krause, MacDonald (October, 1997)